ADVENT

for

EVERYONE

A JOURNEY
THROUGH LUKE

TOM
WRIGHT

First published in Great Britain in 2018

Society for Promoting Christian Knowledge
36 Causton Street
London SW1P 4ST
www.spckpublishing.co.uk

Copyright © Tom Wright 2018

All rights reserved. No part of this book may be reproduced or transmitted
in any form or by any means, electronic or mechanical, including
photocopying, recording, or by any information storage and retrieval
system, without permission in writing from the publisher.

SPCK does not necessarily endorse the individual views
contained in its publications.

The author and publisher have made every effort to ensure that the
external website and email addresses included in this book are correct and
up to date at the time of going to press. The author and publisher are not
responsible for the content, quality or continuing accessibility of the sites.

Scripture quotations are taken or adapted from *The New Testament for
Everyone* by Tom Wright, copyright © Nicholas Thomas Wright 2011.

British Library Cataloguing-in-Publication Data
A catalogue record for this book is available from the British Library

ISBN 978–0–281–07967–4
eBook ISBN 978–0–281–07968–1

1 3 5 7 9 10 8 6 4 2

Typeset by Manila Typesetting Company, Makati City
Printed in Great Britain by CPI

eBook by Manila Typesetting Company, Makati City

Produced on paper from sustainable forests

Tom Wright is Research Professor of New Testament
and Early Christianity at the University of St Andrews.
He is the author of over eighty books, including the For
Everyone guides to the New Testament and, most recently,
Finding God in the Psalms, *The Meal Jesus Gave Us*,
Surprised by Scripture, *Simply Good News*, *God in Public*,
The Day the Revolution Began and *Paul: A Biography* (all
published by SPCK).

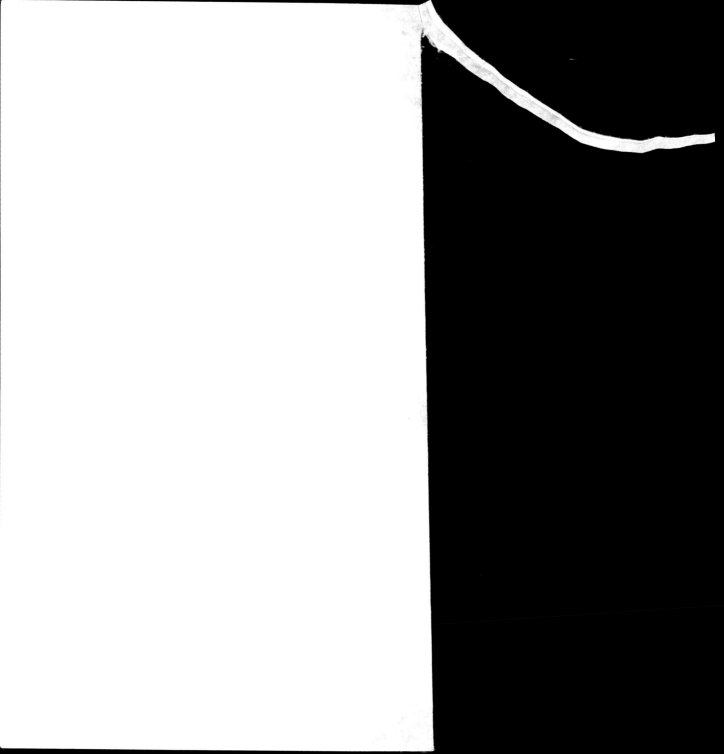

For Scott and Debara Hafemann

CONTENTS

Introduction   xi

WEEK 1: A TIME FOR ENCOURAGEMENT
First Sunday   Watching for the Son of Man
  of Advent   (Luke 21.25–36)   1
Monday   Don't Give Up! (2.41–52)   5
Tuesday   Jesus' Baptism and Genealogy
                  (3.21–38)   9
Wednesday   The Beatitudes (6.12–27)   14
Thursday   Ask and It Will Be Given
                  (11.1–13)   17
Friday   Keep Your Light Shining!
                  (11.29–36)   21
Saturday   Signs of the End (21.5–19)   24

WEEK 2: A TIME FOR RENEWAL
Second Sunday   The Preaching of John the Baptist
  of Advent   (Luke 3.1–6)   30
Monday   The Parable of the Fig Tree
                  (13.1–9)   33
Tuesday   The Parables of the Lost Sheep
                  and the Lost Coin (15.1–10)   37
Wednesday   Teachings on Stewardship
                  (16.10–17)   40

Thursday	The Parable of the Rich Man and Lazarus (16.19–31)	44
Friday	The Rich Young Ruler (18.15–30)	48
Saturday	The Calling of Zacchaeus (19.1–10)	52

Week 3: A Time for Justice

Third Sunday of Advent	John the Baptist Confronts the Crowds (Luke 3.7–18)	56
Monday	Opposition to Jesus in Nazareth (4.14–30)	59
Tuesday	Jesus Sends Out the Seventy (10.1–16)	64
Wednesday	Woes against the Pharisees (11.42–54)	68
Thursday	The Parables of the Persistent Widow and the Tax-Collector (18.1–14)	73
Friday	The Parable of the Tenants (20.9–19)	77
Saturday	David's Son and the Widow's Mite (20.41—21.4)	80

Week 4: A Time for Celebration

Fourth Sunday of Advent	Mary's Song of Praise (Luke 1.39–55)	85
Monday	Zechariah's Song of Praise (1.57–80)	89
Tuesday	The Birth of Jesus (2.1–20)	94
Wednesday	The Celebration of Jesus (10.17–24)	98

CONTENTS

Thursday	The Parable of the Great Banquet (14.12–24)	102
Friday	The Parable of the Prodigal: Part 1 The Father and the Younger Son (15.11–24)	106
Saturday	The Parable of the Prodigal: Part 2 The Father and the Older Son (15.25–32)	110

INTRODUCTION

If people know anything about Advent, they know it's the time when we prepare for Christmas. And when they think of Christmas, they almost always think of Luke. It's Luke that tells us about the angel Gabriel visiting Mary to tell her of God's choice that she should be the mother of his son. It's Luke who has the angels singing to the shepherds in the fields near Bethlehem, and the shepherds then going to find Jesus in the most unlikely place – a manger! – proving that the angels' words had been true. So if Advent is getting ready for Christmas it's also getting ready for Luke.

But Luke can help us with the 'getting ready' as well. Partly this is because he gives us the 'backstory' about John the Baptist, explaining that his birth, too, had been a remarkable act of divine providence. But it's even more, because at various key points Luke explains that what happened to Jesus, and even more importantly what happened *through* Jesus, was the fulfilment of Israel's scriptures. The Bible of the day told a great, sprawling story – of God and the world, God and Israel, God and the hoped-for future. Luke explains that this story reached its appointed goal with Jesus himself. Luke insists that if we want to understand Jesus, and particularly in Advent if we want to understand him better, we have to go back to the Law, the Prophets and the Writings – to the whole ancient scripture of God's people.

In particular, Israel's scriptures were pointing to one great 'arrival'. Many in Jesus' day were expecting a 'Messiah' – a national leader, a warrior king perhaps. But behind and underneath this hope there was a deeper hope again. Prophets like Isaiah and Ezekiel, and in the more recent period prophets like Zechariah and Malachi, had insisted that one day *God himself would come back, to 'visit and redeem his people'*. Luke insists that when we read the story of Jesus this is indeed what we are witnessing, even though the story of Jesus he tells isn't the kind of thing that people had imagined when they thought of the glorious return of Israel's God. Somehow, he is telling us, when Israel's God finally comes back to rescue his people, he comes in the form of this deeply, fully, gloriously human being Jesus of Nazareth. Luke's portrait of Jesus, perhaps more than any of the other gospels, brings out his character as loving, caring, helping, healing – as well as challenging those who dig their toes in and refuse to come onside with God's rescuing project. And Luke insists that *this is what it looks like when God comes back to reign*. This is what Israel had been waiting for. This is what – if it had known its business – the whole world should have been waiting for.

And that brings us to the other side of Advent: because this season isn't just about getting ready for Jesus to be born. It's about getting ready for Jesus to come back. Luke offers a full sweep of global history, from the creation right through to the new creation; and Jesus is the middle of it all. From the moment when Jesus announced in Nazareth that this was the time for God to become king, right through to his resurrection and commissioning of his followers to take his message to the ends of the earth – Luke's story is moving towards the ultimate moment when, as the angel says in Acts chapter 1, Jesus will return at last, to reign over the rescued and renewed creation. This 'second advent' is often not well understood. Different ideas and theories abound. Luke helps us work our way into this set of questions by placing his emphasis on the powerful compassion with which Jesus came alongside and rescued the weak, the helpless, the sick and the hopeless. It is Luke who gives us Jesus' parables of the Good Samaritan and the Prodigal Son. It is Luke who has Jesus meeting a grieving widow and restoring her dead son to life. It is Luke who describes Jesus praying, while being crucified, that God would forgive the men who were torturing him to death.

So Luke is an ideal guide to Advent. The readings for the present book have been chosen to give you a focus for prayer and meditation as you share this journey with other Jesus-followers around the world. With Luke, we find ourselves back in the first century, walking with Jesus along the dusty roads of his homeland, watching with horror as he goes to his death, and then celebrating with astonished joy as he rises to launch God's new world. And with that, Luke will help us return to our own day, to ask humbly and seriously what it will mean for us to walk with Jesus in our own world. My hope and prayer is that this book will help churches, groups and individuals to be 'Advent people', celebrating the coming of God's light into the world that often still seems very dark.

WEEK 1: A TIME FOR ENCOURAGEMENT

FIRST SUNDAY OF ADVENT

Watching for the Son of Man: Luke 21.25–36

[25]'There will be signs in the sun, the moon and the stars. On earth the nations will be in distress and confusion because of the roaring and swelling of the sea and its waves. [26]People will faint from fear, and from imagining all that's going to happen to the world. The powers of the heavens will be shaken. [27]Then they will see "the son of man coming on a cloud" with power and great majesty. [28]When all these things start to happen, stand up and lift up your heads, because the time has come for you to be redeemed.'

[29]He told them this parable. 'Look at the fig tree and all the trees. [30]When they are well into leaf, you can see for yourselves and know that summer is upon you. [31]In the same way, when you see all these things happening, you will know that God's kingdom is upon you. [32]I'm telling you the truth; this generation won't be gone before all of this happens. [33]Heaven and earth may disappear, but these words of mine won't disappear.'

[34]'So watch out for yourselves,' said Jesus, 'that your hearts may not grow heavy with dissipation and drunkenness and the cares of this life, so that that day comes upon you suddenly, like a trap. [35]It will come, you see, on everyone who lives on the face of the earth. [36]Keep awake at all times, praying that you may have strength to escape all these things that will happen, and to stand before the son of man.'

Travel with me, back in time, to Jerusalem. The year is AD 58, nearly 30 years after Jesus' crucifixion and resurrection. Many people in the holy city came to believe in

Jesus in the heady days nearly a generation ago, and many of them are still here, older and more puzzled perhaps, but still waiting and hoping and praying.

Things have been difficult, on and off. Once Pontius Pilate stopped being governor people hoped life might improve, but there was then a huge crisis over the emperor's plan to place a vast statue of himself in the Temple. The threat, fortunately, was seen off; Gaius, the emperor in question, had died soon after; and when one of Herod's grandsons, Agrippa, was made king of the Jews in AD 41, everyone in Jerusalem stood up and cheered. To be ruled by one of your own might be better than having governors from far away who didn't understand local customs. That didn't last, though. He too had died, struck down (said some) by God for blasphemously claiming the sort of divine honours that his pagan masters had given themselves. Now there had been a string of new Roman governors, each one (it seemed) worse than the last. But in 54, when Nero became emperor, many people hoped again that peace and justice would triumph.

All along, though, people in Jerusalem were aware of the political tensions building up. Revolutionary movements arose, had their moment of glory, and were brutally crushed. Some said the priests were secretly involved. Some said it was all the wicked brigands, refusing to let ordinary people go about their business in peace. Some wanted an easy-going peace with Rome, others were all for driving hard bargains, others again wished the Messiah would come. Daily life went on: buying and selling, growing crops, tending herds, woodwork, leatherwork, moneychanging, pottery, with the daily round of Temple sacrifices, music, celebrations and the seasonal feasts as the constant backdrop. The Temple itself was almost complete: the programme of rebuilding begun by Herod the Great 70 years earlier was finally drawing to a close.

And in the middle of all this, those who named the name of Jesus, who still met to break bread and worship in his name, and to teach one another the stories of what he'd done and said, were pulled and pushed this way and that. Some of them were friends of the ex-Pharisee Saul of Tarsus, now known as Paul. He had been here not long ago, and had caused a riot (his friends said his opponents had caused it, but the word on the street was that riots tended to happen wherever Paul went). Now he'd gone, sent to Rome for trial, and he wouldn't be back. Peter, too, had gone on his travels and hadn't been seen for years. Others were sceptical of Paul; he had compromised God's law, they said, allowing Gentiles to worship God through Jesus without demanding circumcision. The leader of the Jerusalem Christians, the wise and devout James, the brother of Jesus himself, was getting older, and his prayers for the redemption of his people didn't seem to be answered.

How easy it was for Jerusalem Christians to become weary! If the gospel was producing exciting results, it was doing so across the sea, and they only heard about it every once in a while, and didn't always like what they heard (Gentiles claiming to worship Jesus but not keeping the law of Moses – that sort of thing). Their lives dragged on day by day. Friends asked them, sometimes unkindly, when this Messiah of theirs was going to reappear, and could he please hurry up because much more of these Romans banging around would bring on a world war, and anyway look what's happened to the price of bread, and if

3

Jesus had really been the Messiah, why has nothing much happened since? Not much use to say that when you met for worship the sense of Jesus' presence and love was so real you could almost reach out and touch him. Not much of an answer to say that you had been told to be patient. Thirty years is a long time. All you could do would be to retell the stories, including the sayings of Jesus such as you find in this passage. Hang on. Be alert. Prop your eyes open – physically, perhaps, spiritually for sure. Pray for strength to meet whatever comes. The son of man will be vindicated, and when he is you want to be on your feet.

Now travel with me to San Francisco, or Sydney, or Bujumbura, or San Salvador, in the twenty-first century. You emerge from the church on Sunday morning – the Pentecostal celebration, the Anglican Matins, the Spanish Mass – and there is the world going about its business, or as it may be its pleasure. Your friends think you're odd still going to church. Everybody knows Christianity is outdated, disproved, boring and irrelevant. What you need is more sex; more parties; more money-making; more revolution. Anyway, hasn't the church done some pretty bad things in its time? What about the Inquisition? (They always say that.) What about the Crusades? Who needs Christianity now that we have computers and space travel? (They said it before about electricity and modern medicine.)

And anyway, they say, if your Jesus is so special, why is the world still in such a mess? They don't want to know about the freeing of the slaves, the rise of education and the building of hospitals; they certainly don't want to know about the lives that are changed every day by the gospel. They want to load you with the cares of this life;

and, as Jesus warned, with dissipation and drunkenness, literal and metaphorical. They want to wear you down, to make you think you're odd and stupid. Why study an old book, they say, that's never done anyone any good?

The answer is the same for us as it was for the Jerusalem Christians nearly a generation after Jesus. Keep alert. This is what you were told to expect. Patience is the key. Pray for strength to keep on your feet. There are times when your eyes will be shutting with tiredness, spiritual, mental, emotional and physical, and when you will have to prop them open. This is what it's about: not an exciting battle, with adrenalin flowing and banners flying, but the steady tread, of prayer and hope and scripture and sacrament and witness, day by day and week by week. This is what counts; this is why patience is a fruit of the spirit. Read the story again. Remind one another of what Jesus said. Encourage one another. And keep awake.

For Reflection or Discussion

Do you ever find yourself growing weary in your journey of faith? What encourages you to keep going?

WEEK 1: MONDAY

Don't Give Up! Luke 2.41–52

[41]Jesus' parents used to go to Jerusalem every year for the Passover festival. [42]When he was twelve years old, they went up as usual for the festival. [43]When the feast days were over, they began the journey back, but the boy Jesus remained in Jerusalem. His parents didn't know; [44]they thought he was in the travelling party, and went a day's journey before looking for him among their relatives and friends.

[45]When they didn't find him, they went back to Jerusalem to look for him. [46]And so it happened that after three days they found him in the Temple, sitting among the teachers, listening to them and asking them questions. [47]Everyone who heard him was astonished at his understanding and his answers.

[48]When they saw him they were quite overwhelmed.

'Child,' said his mother, 'why did you do this to us? Look – your father and I have been in a terrible state looking for you!'

[49]'Why were you looking for me?' he replied. 'Didn't you know that I would have to be getting involved with my father's work?'

[50]They didn't understand what he had said to them. [51]He went down with them and came to Nazareth, and lived in obedience to them. And his mother kept all these things in her heart.

[52]So Jesus became wiser and taller, and gained favour both with God and with the people.

When I was a child, I walked a mile to the bus stop every morning, by myself or with my sister. At the other end of the trip, I walked by myself to school. In the evening, I came back the same way. I never felt unsafe, even in the dark winter days. Now, in many places, children are often taken to school by car. Parents are worried about all kinds of dangers that might be waiting for them.

Perhaps the first remarkable thing about this story is that Mary and Joseph were happy to set off with their large group from Galilee without checking that Jesus was with them. That tells us a lot about the kind of world they lived in, where extended families of kinsfolk and friends lived together in close-knit mutual trust. But, by the same token, once they had left Jerusalem, and when they returned to it by themselves, without the rest of the party, the city was a large and potentially dangerous place, full of dark alleys and strange people, soldiers and traders, not a place where one would be happy to leave one's son for a few days.

The agony of Mary and Joseph, searching for three days, contrasts sharply with the calm response of Jesus when they found him. Mary blurts out an accusation, perhaps tinged with that mixture of guilt and relief that most parents will recognize. Instead of saying, as she might have, 'How could *I* have done this to *you*, leaving you behind like that?', she says, 'How could *you* do this to *us*?' Jesus accepts no blame, and indeed issues a gentle rebuke that speaks volumes, in Luke's portrait, for his own developing self-awareness. 'Your father and I', says Mary, 'have been looking for you.' 'No,' replies Jesus, 'I have been busying myself in my father's work.' Some families today keep notebooks of the striking things their children come out with. Mary kept her notebook in her heart, and this remark in particular will have gone straight there with a stab.

The way Luke has told the story may strike a careful reader of his gospel as part of a large-scale framework around the main story, which is just about to begin. One of the best loved moments in his gospel is the story of the road to Emmaus (24.13–35), in which two disciples are sharing their anguish over the three days that have elapsed since Jesus' death. Jesus meets them, and explains how 'it was necessary that these things had to happen'. Here is another couple, coming back to Jerusalem, finding after three days the Jesus they thought they had lost, and having him explain that 'it was necessary' (the word is the same in Greek) 'that I had to be busy at my father's work'.

You might call the pair of stories something like, 'On Finding the Jesus You Thought You'd Lost'. And if that is the message of these two passages, maybe Luke is wanting to tell us something about his gospel as a whole: maybe he is writing, at one level at least, for people who may have some idea of Jesus but find he is more elusive than they had imagined.

Finding him, of course, will normally involve a surprise. Jesus doesn't do or say what Mary and Joseph, or the two on the road, were expecting. It will be like that with us, too. Every time we relax and think we've really understood him, he will be up ahead, or perhaps staying behind while we go on without thinking. Discipleship always involves the unexpected.

At the heart of the picture, though, is Jesus in the Temple – a theme full of meaning for Luke. The gospel will end with the disciples in the Temple praising God. But, in between this beginning and this end, the Temple, and the holy city which surrounds it, are the subject of some of Jesus' sternest warnings. From now on Jesus will be challenging his contemporaries to make real the promises that go with the Temple. If they don't, the Temple itself will be destroyed.

As we read this story prayerfully, then, we can probably identify quite easily with Mary and Joseph – and perhaps with Jesus, too, quietly asserting an independence of mind and vocation, while still returning home and living in obedience to Mary and Joseph. We may want to remember times when we thought we'd lost someone or something very precious. We may want to reflect on whether we have taken Jesus himself for granted; if Mary and Joseph could do it, there is every reason to suppose that we can too.

We mustn't assume he is accompanying us as we go off on our own business. But if and when we sense the lack of his presence, we must be prepared to hunt for him, to search for him in prayer, in the scriptures, in the sacraments, and not to give up until we find him again.

We must expect, too, that when we do meet him again he will not say or do what we expect. He must be busy with his father's work. So must we.

For Reflection or Discussion

Do you ever feel that you've lost touch with Jesus? If so, what might help you regain and retain a sense of his guiding presence?

WEEK 1: TUESDAY

Jesus' Baptism and Genealogy: Luke 3.21–38

[21]So it happened that, as all the people were being baptized, Jesus too was baptized, and was praying. The heaven was opened, [22]and the holy spirit descended in a bodily form, like a dove, upon him. There came a voice from heaven: 'You are my son, my dear son! I'm delighted with you.'

[23]Jesus was about thirty years old at the start of his work. He was, as people thought, the son of Joseph, from whom his ancestry proceeds back in the following line: Heli, [24]Matthat, Levi, Melchi, Jannai, Joseph, [25]Mattathias, Amos, Nahum, Esli, Naggai, [26]Maath, Mattathias, Semein, Josech, Joda, [27]Johanan, Rhesa, Zerubbabel, Shealtiel, Neri, [28]Melchi, Addi, Kosam, Elmadam, Er, [29]Joshua, Eliezer, Jorim, Matthat, Levi, [30]Simeon, Judah, Joseph, Jonam, Eliakim, [31]Melea, Menna, Mattatha, Nathan, David, [32]Jesse, Obed, Boaz, Sala, Nahshon, [33]Amminadab, Admin, Arni, Hezron, Perez, Judah, [34]Jacob,

Isaac, Abraham, Terah, Nahor, [35]Serug, Reu, Peleg, Eber, Shela, [36]Kainan, Arphachsad, Shem, Noah, Lamech, [37]Methuselah, Enoch, Jared, Mahalaleel, Kainan, [38]Enosh, Seth, Adam, and God.

When I visited New Zealand some years ago, I was taught how to greet an audience in the traditional Maori fashion. I much enjoyed and appreciated the welcome I was given by this ancient people, many of whom are now devout Christians, and the chance to learn something of their history and culture.

Many of the Maori people in New Zealand can tell you which of the original eight long canoes their ancestors arrived in when they first arrived in the country between 800 and 1,000 years ago. There is every reason to suppose that this memory of family trees and origins is reasonably accurate. Many peoples in today's world, and perhaps still more in the ancient world, regularly told and still tell stories of family history, and though these may be embellished from time to time, they are often to be seen as trustworthy. Only in the modern Western world, or where there have been huge social disruptions from war and migration, have people lost touch with ancestry beyond a generation or two.

The Jews were particularly conscious of ancestry, with good reason. God had made promises to Abraham and his family for ever, and through wars, enforced exile, and attempted genocide, they clung (as they still do) to their memories and stories of ancestry as to a lifeline. The books of Chronicles in the Old Testament begin with several chapters of names, which seem very tedious to a modern reader, but were vital for people at the time. They needed to know who they were, which meant knowing which part of the people of Israel they belonged to.

So to begin with it seems surprising that we have not one but two quite different family trees for Jesus. Matthew begins his book with a list of names from Abraham to Jesus; Luke includes a list of names working back from Jesus, through Abraham, to Adam and thence to God himself. And the odd thing is that the lists don't match. Luke has considerably more generations between Abraham and Jesus; and, though some of the stages are the same, the lists part company altogether between David (around 1000 BC) and Salathiel and his son Zerubbabel (after the exile), and then again between Zerubbabel and Joseph. Even the name of Joseph's father is different. In any case, what is the point of a genealogy of *Joseph*, when both Luke and Matthew insist that he was not in fact Jesus' physical father?

Ever since the early days of the church, learned scholars have struggled to give good answers to these questions, and most have admitted defeat. Obviously, in a small and close-knit community, there is every probability that someone could trace their descent from the same source by two or more different routes. The Maori can give several different genealogies for themselves, depending on which ancestor they want to highlight and how much intermarrying has taken place. Different tribal sub-units can trace their descent in different ways for different purposes, resulting in criss-crossing links of all sorts.

This is so even in modern Western society. After my own parents married, they discovered that they were distant cousins, with one remove of generation. Think of the little country of Israel in the period between David and Jesus; similar things could easily have happened. Many could have traced their descent to the same ancestors by at least two routes.

Luke, it seems, has come upon a family tree which he presents without comment, simply to declare that Jesus was indeed not only a true Jew but a descendant of David and Zerubbabel – part of the genuinely royal family. He was counted as Joseph's adopted son, which served, it seems, for this purpose (we are never told whether Mary was of royal descent; since she was a cousin of Elisabeth it may be that she was from a priestly family). If there were other motives in the arrangement of names as they came to Luke (some have suggested that the 77 names should be seen as 11 groups of 7), he doesn't draw our attention to them.

The one link between the family tree and what goes before and comes after is the final phrase: Jesus is the son of God. Of course, by that reckoning so is everyone else in the list, from Joseph right back to Adam. Luke certainly means more than this when he uses the phrase 'son of God' as a title for Jesus (1.35; 3.22; 4.3, 9). Perhaps it is best to see the family tree, stretching back to the creation of the world, as a way of saying that, though Jesus is indeed the Messiah of Israel (another meaning of 'son of God'), he is so precisely for the whole world. All creation, the whole human race, will benefit from what he has come to do.

This global scope to God's purposes is in the background as Jesus comes to the Jordan to be baptized by John. Luke adds here, as in one or two other key points, the fact that Jesus was praying when the crucial revelation occurred. Part of his constant picture of Jesus is that he was a man of prayer. It's often suggested that the baptism was the moment when Jesus received his first inkling of a messianic calling, but this can hardly be correct; the voice from heaven comes to confirm and give direction to something that has been true all along, as Luke has already told us (2.49). The spirit and the word together give Jesus the encouragement and strength he needs to begin his short public career.

They also give an indication of where that career will take him. The heavenly voice echoes words of Isaiah the prophet (42.1), commissioning the Messiah as the Servant, the one who will suffer and die for the people and the world. Behind that again are echoes of Genesis 22.2, when Abraham was commanded to kill his beloved only son, Isaac. The voice is at the same time a wonderful affirmation of Jesus' vocation and a clear reminder of where it is to lead.

Together the baptism story and the family tree tell us where Jesus has come from, who he is, and where he is going. As we make his story our own in our own prayers, and indeed in our own baptism, we too should expect both the fresh energy of the spirit and the quiet voice which reminds us of God's amazing, encouraging love and of the path of vocation which lies ahead.

For Reflection or Discussion

How clear is your vision of the spiritual path ahead of you? How might reflecting on the experience of Jesus help you to see it more clearly?

WEEK 1: WEDNESDAY

The Beatitudes: Luke 6.12–27

[12]It happened around that time that Jesus went up into the mountain to pray, and he spent all night in prayer to God. [13]When day came, he called his disciples, and chose twelve of them, calling them 'apostles': [14]Simon, whom he called Peter, and Andrew his brother, and James and John, and Philip, Bartholomew, [15]Matthew, Thomas, James son of Alphaeus, Simon who was called 'the hothead', [16]Judas son of James, and Judas Iscariot, who turned traitor.

[17]He went down with them, and took up a position on a level plain where there was a large crowd of his followers, with a huge company of people from all Judaea, from Jerusalem, and from the coastal region of Tyre and Sidon. [18]They came to hear him, and to be cured from their diseases. Those who were troubled by unclean spirits were healed, [19]and the whole crowd tried to touch him, because power was going out from him and healing everybody.

[20]He lifted up his eyes and looked at his disciples, and said:

'Blessings on the poor: God's kingdom belongs to you!
[21]'Blessings on those who are hungry today: you'll have a feast!
'Blessings on those who weep today: you'll be laughing!
[22]'Blessings on you, when people hate you, and shut you out, when they slander you and reject your name as if it was evil, because of the son of man. [23]Celebrate on that day!
Jump for joy! Don't you see: in heaven there is a great reward for you! That's what your ancestors did to the prophets.
[24]'But woe betide you rich: you've had your comfort!
[25]'Woe betide you if you're full today: you'll go hungry!

14

²⁶'Woe betide you if you're laughing today: you'll be mourning and weeping!
²⁷'Woe betide you when everyone speaks well of you: that's what your ancestors did to the false prophets.'

Let us imagine that you are a schoolteacher. One day, you go out into the school playground, where there are dozens of children kicking footballs around. You go over to where they are, and call for them to gather round. Then you begin, slowly but surely, to select eleven of them. You don't need to say a word. Choose your 11 and lead them off somewhere else. Everyone will know what you're doing. You're picking a football team.

Then suppose you and your team begin to work together, to train for the serious games ahead. What are you going to do? You assume they know something of football, something of the rules. But you want to tell them that some things are quite different now. The game has changed. Things you do in the playground aren't the same as things you do in a real match.

But it's no good lecturing them for hours about how to play. What they need is three or four things to remember to do, and three or four things to remember *not* to do. Then, in the heat of the moment, these basic guidelines will come back to them and encourage them to stay focused on how best to play the game.

Now think what Jesus was doing. They didn't have football teams in his day, and in any case what he was doing was far more serious than that. What they did have was a long memory of the time when God called the 12 tribes of Israel – descended from the 12 sons of Jacob – and made them his special people, so that through them he could fulfil his purposes for the whole world. Now Jesus has come, as it were, out onto the playground where all sorts of people are trying out ways of being God's people – some with new rules to obey, some with new schemes for violent revolution, some with support for Herod and his regime, some with proposals for withdrawing into the desert and praying in private, and no doubt others as well. From the people he has met, he chooses 12. Even if he'd done that without a word, everyone could see what he was doing. He was picking an Israel team. They were to be the nucleus, the centre and starting-point, for what God was now going to do. They were the core of God's renewed Israel.

He gave them clear orders as to how his vision of God's work would go forward. Four promises, and four warnings, presented in terms of Israel's great scriptural codes: in the book called Deuteronomy, there were long lists of 'blessings' for those who obeyed the law, and 'curses' for those who didn't. These formed part of the charter, the covenant, the binding agreement between God and Israel. Now, with the renewed Israel formed around him, Jesus gives them his own version of the same thing.

And a radical version it is. It's an upside-down code, or perhaps (Jesus might have said) a right-way-up code instead of the upside-down ones people had been following. God is doing something quite new: he is fulfilling his promises at last, and this will mean good news and encouragement for all the people who haven't had any for a long time. The poor, the hungry, those who weep, those who are hated: blessings on them! Not that there's anything virtuous about being poor or hungry in itself. But when injustice is reigning, the world will have to be turned once more the right way up for God's justice and kingdom to come to birth. And that will provoke opposition from people who like things the way they are. Jesus' message of promise and warning, of blessing and curse, rang with echoes of the Hebrew prophets of old, and he knew that the reaction would be the same.

As Christians we believe that what Jesus began with the call of the Twelve and the sharp-edged teaching of blessings and curses remains in force today. This is the shape of the kingdom: the kingdom which still today turns the world upside down, or perhaps the right way up, as much as ever it did.

For Reflection or Discussion

What are the tasks to which Jesus is calling his church today? What are his promises and warnings for those who will hear his call and follow him?

WEEK 1: THURSDAY

Ask and It Will Be Given: Luke 11.1–13

[1]Once Jesus was praying in a particular place. When he had finished, one of his disciples approached.

'Teach us to pray, Master,' he said, 'just like John taught his disciples.'

[2]'When you pray,' replied Jesus, 'this is what to say:

'Father, may your name be honoured; may your kingdom come; [3]give us each day our daily bread; [4]and forgive us our sins, since we too forgive all our debtors; and don't put us to the test.

[5]'Suppose one of you has a friend,' he said, 'and you go to him in the middle of the night and say, "My dear friend,

lend me three loaves of bread! [6]A friend of mine is on a journey and has arrived at my house, and I have nothing to put in front of him!" [7]He will answer from inside his house, "Don't make life difficult for me! The door is already shut, and my children and I are all in bed! I can't get up and give you anything." [8]Let me tell you, even if he won't get up and give you anything just because you're his friend, because of your shameless persistence he will get up and give you whatever you need.

[9]'So this is my word to you: ask and it will be given you; search and you will find; knock and it will be opened to you. [10]You see, everyone who asks receives! Everyone who searches finds! Everyone who knocks has the door opened for them! [11]If your son asks you for a fish, is there a father among you who will give him a snake? [12]Or if he asks for an egg, will you give him a scorpion? [13]Face it: you are evil. And yet you know how to give good presents to your children. How much more will your heavenly father give the holy spirit to those who ask him!'

The telephone rang. It was a message that my younger son, a singer, was about to get on an aeroplane to go with his choir to the other side of the world. If I was quick, I might just be able to catch him with a call to wish him well. I phoned, caught him, and we had a good chat. There are times when I wonder where fatherhood ends and friendship begins.

Friendship and fatherhood together teach us something about God and prayer. Actually, the learning can be a two-way street. It isn't just a matter of thinking about earthly friends and fathers and then learning that God is like that. There are times when a father needs to take a long, hard look at what God's fatherhood is all about, and start changing his own fatherhood behaviour to be more like it. And most of our friendships, I suspect, could do with the improvement that some reflection about God as a friend might provide.

It is that picture – of God as a friend, in bed and asleep, with his children around him – which probably strikes us as the more peculiar. (We are used to saying that God is our father, though we may not always ask what exactly that means; but God as our Friend is less obvious.) In the sort of house Jesus has in mind, the family would all sleep side by side on the floor, so that if the father got up at midnight the whole family would be woken up. My children are now past that stage (my wife and I are more likely to be woken up when they come home at midnight or later), but it's obvious what a nuisance it is when the knock comes on the door.

Yet the friend outside has a real problem, and the sleeping friend can and will help him. The laws of hospitality in the ancient Middle East were strict, and if a traveller arrived needing food and shelter one was under an obligation to provide them. The friend in the street knows that the friend in bed will understand; he would do the same if the roles were reversed.

What counts is *persistence*. There are all sorts of ways in which God isn't like a sleepy friend, but Jesus is focusing on one point of comparison only: he is encouraging a kind of holy boldness, a sharp knocking on the door, an insistent asking, a search that refuses to give up. That's what our prayer should be like. This isn't just a routine or formal praying, going through the motions as a daily or weekly task. There is a battle on, a fight with the powers of darkness, and those who have glimpsed the light are called to struggle in prayer – for peace, for reconciliation, for wisdom, for a thousand things for the world and the church, perhaps a hundred or two for one's own family, friends and neighbours, and perhaps a dozen or two for oneself.

There are, of course, too many things to pray about. That's why it's important to be disciplined and regular. If you leave it to the whim of the moment you'll never be a true intercessor, somebody through whose prayers God's love is poured out into the world. But because these things are urgent, important and complex there has to be more to prayer than simply discipline and regularity. Formal prayers, including official liturgies for services in church, are vital for most people for their spiritual health, but they are like the metal shell of a car. To be effective it needs fuel for its engine, and to be effective prayers need energy, too: in this case, the kind of dogged and even funny determination that you'd use with a sleepy friend who you hoped would help you out of a tight spot.

The larger picture, though, is the more familiar one of God as father. This isn't just an illustration drawn from family life, though of course it is that at its heart, and Jesus' illustrations about giving a child real food rather than poisonous snakes make their point. If we are ever tempted to imagine God as a tyrant who would take delight in giving us things that weren't good for us, we should remember these pictures and think again. But the illustration is bigger than that as well. The idea of God as father goes right back to the time when Israel was in slavery and needed rescuing. 'Israel is my son, my firstborn,' declared God to Pharaoh through Moses and Aaron;

'so let my people go!' From then on, to call on God as 'father' was to invoke the God of the exodus, the liberating God, the God whose kingdom was coming, bringing bread for the hungry, forgiveness for the sinner, and deliverance from the powers of darkness.

For Reflection or Discussion

Do you need encouraging to pray more regularly or more often? If so, what lifestyle changes might you make in order to facilitate that?

WEEK 1: FRIDAY

Keep Your Light Shining! Luke 11.29–36

[29]The crowds kept increasing. Jesus began to say to them, 'This generation is an evil generation! It looks for a sign, and no sign will be given to it except the sign of Jonah.

[30]'Jonah was a sign to the people of Nineveh; just so, the son of man will be a sign to this generation. [31]The Queen of the South will rise up in the judgment with the men of this generation and will condemn them: she came from the ends of the earth to listen to Solomon's wisdom, and look – something greater than Solomon is here. [32]The men of Nineveh will rise up in the judgment with this generation and will condemn it: they repented at Jonah's preaching, and look – something greater than Jonah is here.

[33]'Nobody lights a lamp in order to hide it or put it under a jug. They put it on a lampstand, so that people who come in can see the light.

[34]'Your eye is the lamp of your body. If your eye is focused, your whole body is full of light. But if it's evil, your body is in darkness. [35]Watch out, then, in case the light inside you turns

21

to darkness. ³⁶If your whole body is illuminated, with no part in darkness, everything will be illuminated, just as you are by a flash of lightning.'

The great church is completely dark. It is almost midnight, and the little crowd outside the west door shuffles round and stamps to keep warm in the chilly April air. Then, as the clock strikes, the fire is lit, with a sudden glow on all the watching faces. A single candle is lit from the fire. The doors swing open, the light moves forward into the pitch-black church, and the Easter celebration begins. Soon the whole place will be full of flickering, glowing candlelight, the light of God's power and love shining in the darkness of the world.

Not every church celebrates Easter this way, but those that do will have no difficulty making the connections that hold together the rather confusing collection of sayings in this passage. The context is still, of course, Jesus' journey to Jerusalem, like a candle going forward into the darkness.

When the light comes, it scatters the darkness; but what if you were rather enjoying the darkness, able to get on unseen with whatever evil purposes you had? Light brings hope and new possibility, but it also brings judgment. Light symbolizes new life in the face of the darkness of death, but it also shows up that darkness for what it is. These sayings, then, though full of hope, are also filled with warnings of judgment. Jesus, on his way to Jerusalem, is constantly saying in one way or another that God's light will shine out and expose the darkness that had taken hold of the hearts and minds of his contemporaries.

It all begins with a sign – the sign of Jonah. Jonah is an almost comic figure in the Old Testament: the prophet who runs away, the problem passenger thrown into the sea, the dinner the whale can't stomach, and the hot-head who gets cross with God over a withered plant. In between, though, he told the people of Nineveh to repent, never thinking they would listen and obey. But he was wrong: they did – whether or not, as in Matthew's version of the story, because they had heard about his escapade with the sea and the whale, or whether simply because of the power of the message.

Now here is Jesus, anything but a comic figure, telling his own people it's time to repent, and they ignore him. Here is Jesus with a greater wisdom than even the legendary Solomon, and his own people don't listen. There is a straight line from this point that leads to the moment when Jesus weeps over Jerusalem because, unlike Nineveh, it has ignored the warnings, refused the way of peace, and thereby sealed its own fate.

Luke's reader, meanwhile, is left to ponder the way in which Jesus speaks of the foreigners, the Queen of the South and the people of Nineveh, who will 'rise at the judgment'. The two words used to mean 'rise' are both regular early Christian words for the resurrection: Luke expects his readers to know about the coming resurrection of the dead, and of the great judgment that will then take place. The light of Easter is the light of judgment as well as hope.

When we read the sayings about light, then, they speak of more than a general wisdom or spiritual illumination. To begin with, Jesus warns that the light that has come into the midst of Israel is designed not to remain hidden but to shine all around. Then, changing the image, he gives another warning, more cryptic for us and easy to miss.

To begin with, it looks like a rather obvious saying ⸱ human life: 'If the eye is in working order,' Jesus see. be saying, 'you can see where you're going; but if it you can't; so watch out in case your light (that is, yo⸱ becomes darkened.' Now clearly Jesus isn't givir about protecting our physical eyes; nor about itual dangers of looking at the wrong things. Nor, ⸱ is he just speaking of the spiritual insight of indiv⸱⸱ ⸱⸱s. The passage makes more sense, especially where Luke has placed it, as a warning to 'this generation', his contemporaries. They must watch out in case they fail to see the light that was standing there in their midst.

The final sentence is then an encouragement to embrace and live by the light while there's time. A day is coming when everything will be lit up (compare 17.24), and on that day those who have allowed the light to illuminate them fully will shine brightly.

For Reflection or Discussion

The light of Christ has been in the world for 2,000 years. Are we any better at embracing it for ourselves than Jesus' contemporaries were? What are you doing to shine his light in the world so that others may come to embrace it too?

WEEK 1: SATURDAY

Signs of the End: Luke 21.5–19

[5]Some people were talking about the Temple, saying how wonderfully it was decorated, with its beautiful stones and dedicated gifts.

said Jesus; [6]'but the days will come when everything will be torn down. Not one stone will be left standing on the other.'

'a er,' they asked him, 'when will these things happen? w be the sign that it's all about to take place?'

' out that nobody deceives you,' said Jesus. 'Yes: l   of people will come using my name, saying "I'm the one!" and "The time has come!" Don't go following them. [9]When you hear about wars and rebellions, don't be alarmed. These things have to happen first, but the end won't come at once.

[10]'One nation will rise against another,' he went on, 'and one kingdom against another. [11]There will be huge earthquakes, famines and plagues in various places, terrifying omens, and great signs from heaven.

[12]'Before all this happens they will lay hands on you and persecute you. They will hand you over to the synagogues and prisons. They will drag you before kings and governors because of my name. [13]That will become an opportunity for you to tell your story. [14]So settle it in your hearts not to work out beforehand what tale to tell; [15]I'll give you a mouth and wisdom, which none of your opponents will be able to resist or contradict.

[16]'You will be betrayed by parents, brothers and sisters, relatives and friends, and they will kill some of you. [17]You will be hated by everyone because of my name. [18]But no hair of your head will be lost. [19]The way to keep your lives is to be patient.'

A news reader announces that an asteroid passed close to the earth. When they say 'close', they mean about half a million miles; but in terms of the solar system, that's quite near at hand. It shows, as one commentator said, that the planet Earth is in a bit of a shooting gallery. If I had lived in ancient Greece, or Rome or Egypt, instead of being in the modern world, with efficient telescopes watching, and well-trained scientists ready to explain everything they see, the sight of a strange, moving light in part of the sky where there hadn't been anything before would at once have been seized upon as a sign. Something dramatic was going to happen.

These near misses happen about once a century. Of course, if the asteroid had hit the earth, something dramatic would have happened all right; not only would it make a hole nearly a mile across, but the energy released as it did so would be the equivalent of several atom bombs. No question of the significance of that.

But in Jesus' day dramatic and unexpected happenings in the night sky were often thought to signify more than just physical disaster as large objects crashed to earth. People looked at them carefully because they believed they would tell them about the imminent rise and fall of kings and empires. And when Jesus' disciples asked him how they would know when the frightening events he was talking about would take place, that's probably the sort of thing they had in mind. Surely Jesus would want them to know, and so would give them signs to watch out for?

Jesus will give them signs of a sort, but actually the main thing he wants them to learn is that there will be a period of waiting, when they will have to be patient through dangerous and testing times.

But what great event will they be waiting for? Luke, more than all the other gospels, has prepared us for the answer. His alert readers will not be surprised at Jesus' prediction. The Temple, the most beautiful building one could imagine, adorned and decorated by the skill and love of hundreds of years, and occupying the central place in the national life, religion and imagination – the Temple itself would be torn down. It had come to stand for the perversion of Israel's call that Jesus had opposed throughout his public career. If he was right, the present Temple was wrong; if God was to vindicate him, that would have to include the Temple's destruction. This was as unthinkable for a devout Jew as it would be for an American to imagine the destruction of the White House, the Washington Memorial and the Statue of Liberty; only much more so, because the Temple signified a thousand years of God's dealings with Israel.

Jesus' warnings about what the disciples will face in the days to come clearly indicate that he will no longer be with them, but that they will still be marked out as his followers. Others will come pretending to be him, or to be his spokesperson. The world will be convulsed with wars and revolutions, all the more alarming because, without radio, television, telephones or newspapers, people would hear of such things by rumour from travellers, and would pass on the news with additional speculation until a border skirmish had been inflated, in the telling, to become an all-out war, and the emperor's occasional sneeze had been exaggerated into a fatal illness.

Jesus clearly expects that amid these turbulent times his followers will be marked out as undesirables. People would retain a memory of Jesus as someone leading Israel astray, deflecting people from keeping the law, and from defending the national interest, with his dangerous talk of God's kingdom, of peace and grace for all. When the going got tough, in Israel and in Jewish communities around the world, those who were known as Jesus' people would be in the firing line; and, quite soon, non-Jewish communities would follow their example. Families would be split; sometimes it would seem that the Christians were the ones blamed for everything, the ones everybody loved to hate. If ever they needed patience, they would need it then.

Jesus promises, though, that he will give them what they need during this time of waiting: 'a mouth and wisdom'. This promise should not, of course, be taken as licence to ignore the hard work required for regular Christian teaching. It refers to the times when people are on trial for their lives because of their allegiance to Jesus. The story of the first generation of Christianity – the time between the resurrection of Jesus and the fall of the Temple in AD 70 – bears out these prophecies. And many early Christians would testify that Jesus had indeed been with them and given them words to say.

But this passage, though vital in its specific reference to that first generation, has a good deal to say to the subsequent church as well. Wherever Christians are persecuted for their faith – and, sadly but not surprisingly, this is still common in many parts of the world – they need not only the prayers and support of their fellow believers in more fortunate places, but also the comfort and encouragement of these words: 'Don't let anyone deceive you'; 'a chance to tell your story'; 'I'll give you wisdom'; 'you'll keep your lives through patience'. These are still precious promises, to be learnt ahead of time and clung to in the moment of need.

For Reflection or Discussion

What are you doing to support and encourage fellow Christians who are being persecuted in other parts of the world? How can you find out how you can help, and encourage others to do the same?

WEEK 2: A TIME FOR RENEWAL

SECOND SUNDAY OF ADVENT

The Preaching of John the Baptist: Luke 3.1–6

[1]It was the fifteenth year of the reign of Tiberius Caesar. Pontius Pilate was governor of Judaea; Herod was Tetrarch of Galilee; his brother Philip was tetrarch of Ituraea and Trachonitis; Lysanias was tetrarch of Abilene. [2]Annas and Caiaphas were the high priests.

At that time, the word of God came to John, the son of Zechariah, in the wilderness. [3]He went through all the region of the Jordan, announcing a baptism of repentance for the forgiveness of sins. [4]This is what is written in the book of the words of Isaiah the prophet:

A voice shouting in the wilderness:
Get ready a path for the Lord,
Make the roads straight for him!
[5]Every valley shall be filled in,
And every mountain and hill shall be flattened,
The twisted paths will be straightened out,
And the rough roads smoothed off,
[6]And all that lives shall see God's rescue.

Imagine massive floods sweeping through the country-side. Ancient cities suddenly find themselves under several feet of water. People aren't expecting it, and now can't quite believe it's happening.

If the authorities have enough warning, they do their best to get people out of their houses to stop them being trapped. They drive round parts of the city announcing that trouble is approaching and that people should leave at once. They make announcements on the local radio and television. Imminent danger needs urgent action.

That's the kind of work John the Baptist was doing. We don't usually think of preachers going around making that kind of announcement. Even politicians don't usually tell us things are getting very urgent – or, if they do, we usually take no notice. But people believed John, and came to him for a different sort of flooding: baptism, being plunged into the river Jordan.

What was the emergency, and how would being plunged in the Jordan help people to avoid danger?

Luke's introduction to the story of John the Baptist is designed to give us a fairly precise date when it all happened, but actually it gives us a lot more besides. Behind the list of names and places is a story of oppression and misery that was building up to explosion point.

Rome had ruled the area for about a hundred years, but only since AD 6 had there been a Roman governor resident in the area, living in Caesarea (on the Mediterranean coast) but also keeping a base in Jerusalem. Augustus Caesar, the first emperor, had died in AD 14, and his place had been taken by the ruthless Tiberius, who was already being worshipped as a god in the eastern parts of the empire. Two of Herod the Great's sons, Herod Antipas and Philip, were ruling somewhat shakily, under Roman permission, in the north of the country, but Rome had taken direct control of the south, including Jerusalem itself. Most Jews didn't regard Herod's sons as real rulers; they were a self-made royal house, ruling, like Rome, by fear and oppression. The high priests weren't much better. Popular movements of resistance had come and gone, in some cases being brutally put down. Everybody knew they couldn't go on as they were. Something had to happen. But what?

Devout Jews had longed for a new word from God. Some believed that prophecy had died out but might one day be revived. Many expected that a movement would begin through which their God would renew the age-old covenant, bringing Israel out of slavery into a new freedom. The old prophets had spoken of a time of renewal, through which God himself would come back to them. They had only a sketchy idea of what this would all look like, but when a fiery young prophet appeared in the Judaean wilderness, going round the towns and villages telling people that the time had come, they were ready to listen.

Baptism, plunging into the river Jordan, was a powerful sign of this renewal. When the children of Israel had come out of Egypt – a story they all knew well because of their regular Passovers and other festivals – they were brought through the Red Sea, through the Sinai wilderness, then through the Jordan into the promised land. Now they were in slavery again – in their own land! – and wanted a new exodus to bring them to freedom. Since the old prophets had declared that this slavery was the result of Israel's sin, worshipping idols rather than their one true God, the new exodus, when it happened, would have to deal with this. The way to escape slavery, the prophets had said, was to 'return' to God with heart and soul; that is, to 'repent'. 'Return to me, and I will return to you,' one of the last prophets had said (Malachi 3.7).

Hence John's agenda: 'a baptism of repentance for the forgiveness of sins'. John was doing what the prophet Isaiah had said: preparing a pathway for the Lord himself to return to his people. This was the time. Rescue was at hand.

For Reflection or Discussion

Can you think of anything you need to repent of and change in your life of Christian discipleship? What might help you to make that change and make it stick?

WEEK 2: MONDAY

The Parable of the Fig Tree: Luke 13.1–9

[1]At that moment some people came up and told them the news. Some Galileans had been in the Temple, and Pilate had mixed their blood with that of the sacrifices.

[2]'Do you suppose', said Jesus, 'that those Galileans suffered such things because they were greater sinners than all other Galileans? [3]No, let me tell you! Unless you repent, you will all be destroyed in the same way.

[4]'And what about those eighteen who were killed when the tower in Siloam collapsed on top of them? Do you imagine they were more blameworthy than everyone else who lives in Jerusalem? [5]No, let me tell you! Unless you repent, you will all be destroyed in the same way.'

[6]He told them this parable. 'Once upon a time there was a man who had a fig tree in his vineyard. He came to it looking for fruit, and didn't find any. [7]So he said to the gardener, "Look here! I've been coming to this fig tree for three years hoping to find some fruit, and I haven't found any! Cut it down! Why should it use up the soil?"

[8]'"I tell you what, Master," replied the gardener; "let it alone for just this one year more. I'll dig all round it and put on some manure. [9]Then, if it fruits next year, well and good; and if not, you can cut it down."'

If the New Testament had never been written, we would still know that Pontius Pilate was an unpleasant and unpopular governor of Judaea. The Jewish historian Josephus lists several things he did which upset and irritated the local Jewish population. Sometimes he seemed to be deliberately trying to make them angry. He trampled on their religious sensibilities; once he tried to bring Roman standards (military emblems) into Jerusalem, with their pagan symbols. He flouted their laws and conventions; once he used money from the Temple treasury to build an aqueduct, and then brutally crushed the rebellion that resulted. These incidents, and others like them, are recorded outside the New Testament, and help us to understand what sort of person Pilate was.

So it shouldn't surprise us to learn that on another occasion, while some people on pilgrimage from Galilee had been offering sacrifice in the Temple, Pilate sent the troops in, perhaps fearing a riot, and slaughtered them. The present passage simply speaks of their own blood mingling in the Temple courtyard with the blood of their sacrifices – polluting the place, on top of the human horror and tragedy of such an event. It is as though occupying forces were to invade a church and butcher worshippers on Christmas Day.

Remind yourself for a moment where we are in Luke's story. Jesus has decided to go to Jerusalem at the head of a party of Galilean pilgrims. If today I was planning a journey to a town under enemy occupation, and was told on the way there that the local governor was making a habit of killing visiting English clergymen, I suspect I would call my travel agent and book a flight to somewhere less dangerous.

These people, then, aren't simply bringing Jesus information. Two questions hover in the air as they tell their shocking news. First, does Jesus really intend to continue his journey? Isn't he afraid of what may happen to him there? And second, what does this mean? Is this the beginning of something worse? If Jesus has been warning of woe and disaster coming on those who refuse his message, is this a sign that these Galileans were already being punished? Jesus' stern comments address the second of these questions. (The first remains in the air throughout the chapter, until finally (13.31–35) we discover the answer: Herod is out to kill Jesus in Galilee, but Jesus knows that he must get to Jerusalem. Nowhere is now safe.) Yes, Pilate has killed Galilean pilgrims in Jerusalem; but they were no more sinful than any other Galilean pilgrims. Rather – and he is about to repeat the point – *unless you repent, you will all be destroyed the same way.*

The same way? That's the key. Jesus isn't talking about what happens to people after they die. Many have read this passage and supposed that it was a warning about perishing in hell after death, but that is clearly wrong. In line with the warnings he has issued several times already, and will continue to issue right up to his own crucifixion, Jesus is making it clear that those who refuse his summons to change direction, to abandon the crazy flight into national rebellion against Rome, will suffer the consequences. Those who take the sword will perish with the sword.

Or, if not the sword, they will be crushed by buildings in Jerusalem as the siege brings them crashing down. Siloam is a small area of Jerusalem, close to the centre of the ancient city, just to the south of the Temple itself. Building accidents happen; but if the Jerusalemites continue to refuse God's kingdom-call to repent, to turn from their present agendas, then those who escape Roman swords will find the very walls collapsing on top of them as the enemy closes in.

This terrifying warning, about the political and military consequences of not heeding his call, is at once amplified by the almost humorous, yet in fact quite sinister, parable of the fig tree in the vineyard. (People often planted fig trees in vineyards; it was good for the grapes.) Underneath the banter between the vineyard-owner and the gardener we detect a direct comment on Jesus' own ministry, and a further answer as to what's going to happen when he gets to Jerusalem.

There are two ways of taking the story, both of which give a satisfactory meaning and arrive at the same point. Jesus himself could be seen as the vineyard-owner. He has been coming to the Lord's garden, seeking the fruit of repentance, throughout his ministry. (We might take the 'three years' of 13.7 as an indication that Jesus' ministry had lasted that long, but it's more likely that it is simply part of the logic of the story.) So far, apart from a very few followers, who are themselves still quite muddled, he has found none: no repentance, not even in the cities where most of his mighty deeds had been done (10.13–15). He is prepared, then, to give Israel, and particularly Jerusalem, the Temple, and the ruling priests one more chance. If they still refuse, their doom will be sealed.

Or maybe it is God who has been coming to Israel these many years, seeking fruit. Maybe Jesus is the gardener, the servant who is now trying, as the owner's patience wears thin, to dig around and put on manure, to inject new life and health into the old plant before sentence is passed. Either way the end result is the same: 'If not, you can cut it down.' Luke's arrangement of the material from chapter 10 onwards leaves us in no doubt as to how he saw the matter: when Jerusalem fell in AD 70, it was a direct result of refusing to follow the way of peace which Jesus had urged throughout his ministry.

For Reflection or Discussion

What do Christians need to repent of most urgently today? Are you bearing fruit for God's kingdom, or are you spending more time and energy in pursuing other agendas?

WEEK 2: TUESDAY

The Parables of the Lost Sheep and the Lost Coin: Luke 15.1–10

[1]All the tax-collectors and sinners were coming close to listen to Jesus. [2]The Pharisees and the legal experts were grumbling. 'This fellow welcomes sinners!' they said. 'He even eats with them!'

[3]So Jesus told them this parable. [4]"Supposing one of you has a hundred sheep,' he said, 'and you lose one of them. What will you do? Why, you'll leave the ninety-nine out in the countryside, and you'll go off looking for the lost one until you find it! [5]And when you find it, you'll be so happy – you'll put it on your shoulders [6]and come home, and you'll call your friends and neighbours in. "Come and have a party!" you'll say. "Celebrate with me! I've found my lost sheep!"

[7]"Well, let me tell you: that's how glad they will be in heaven over one sinner who repents – more than over ninety-nine righteous people who don't need repentance.

[8]"Or supposing a woman has ten drachmas and loses one of them. What will she do? Why, she'll light a lamp, and sweep the house, and hunt carefully until she finds it! [9]And when she

finds it she'll call her friends and neighbours in. "Come and have a party!" she'll say. "Celebrate with me! I've found my lost coin!"

[10]'Well, let me tell you: that's how glad God's angels feel when a single sinner repents.'

We had just moved house, to a dream location: quiet, secluded, at the end of a road near a lake. Everything seemed peaceful. Then, on the first Saturday night we were there, all chaos broke loose. Loud music, amplified voices making announcements, cheers, fireworks – all going on well into the small hours, keeping our young children awake. We were appalled. Was this going to happen every weekend? Where was the noise coming from? Why had nobody told us about this before we bought the house?

In the morning, the explanations came. No, it wasn't a regular occurrence. It would only happen once a year. It was the local Yacht Club's annual party, celebrating some great event in the sailing calendar. We returned to tranquillity. But it left me thinking about how one person's celebration can be really annoying for someone else, especially if they don't understand the reason for the party.

The three parables in Luke 15 are told because Jesus was making a habit of having celebration parties with all the 'wrong' people, and some others thought it was a nightmare. All three stories are ways of saying: 'This is why we're celebrating! Wouldn't you have a party if it was you? How could we not?' In and through them all we get a wide-open window on what Jesus thought he was doing – and, perhaps, on what we ourselves should be doing.

At the heart of the trouble was the character of the people Jesus was eating with on a regular basis. The tax-collectors were disliked not just because they were tax-collectors – nobody much likes them in any culture – but because they were collecting money for either Herod or the Romans, or both, and nobody cared for them at all. And if they were in regular contact with Gentiles, some might have considered them unclean.

The 'sinners' are a more general category, and people disagree as to who precisely they were. They may just have been people who were too poor to know the law properly or to try to keep it (see John 7.49). Certainly they were people who were regarded by the self-appointed experts as hopelessly irreligious, out of touch with the demands that God had made on Israel through the law.

Throughout the chapter Jesus is *not* saying that such people were simply to be accepted as they stand. Sinners must repent and renew their lives by becoming more closely attuned to God. Jesus has a different idea from his critics of what 'repentance' means. For them, nothing short of adopting their standards of purity and law-observance would do. For Jesus, when people follow him and his way, that is the true repentance. And – he doesn't say so in so many words, but I think it's there by implication – the Pharisees and legal experts themselves need to repent in that way. 'Righteous persons who don't need to repent' indeed (verse 7)! Try saying the sentence with a smile and a question-mark in your voice and you will, I think, hear what Jesus intended.

The point of the parables is then clear. This is why there's a party going on: all heaven is having a party, the angels are joining in, and if we don't have one as well we'll be out of tune with God's reality.

In the stories of the sheep and the coin, the punch line in each case depends on the Jewish belief that the two halves of God's creation, heaven and earth, were meant to fit together and be in harmony with each other. If you discover what's going on in heaven, you'll discover how things were meant to be on earth. That, after all, is the point of praying that God's kingdom will come 'on earth as in heaven'. As far as the legal experts and Pharisees were concerned, the closest you could get to heaven was in the Temple; the Temple required strict purity from the priests; and the closest that non-priests could get to copying heaven was to maintain a similarly strict purity in every aspect of life. But now Jesus was declaring that heaven was having a great, noisy party every time a single sinner saw the light and began to follow God's way. If earth-dwellers wanted to copy the life of heaven, they'd have a party too. That's what Jesus was doing.

For Reflection or Discussion

Do you or your church need to find more sources of renewal? What might need to change in order for you to become more closely attuned to hearing and doing God's will 'on earth as in heaven'?

WEEK 2: WEDNESDAY

Teachings on Stewardship: Luke 16.10–17

[10]'Someone who is faithful in a small matter', Jesus continued, 'will also be faithful in a large one. Someone who is dishonest

in a small matter will also be dishonest in a large one. [11]If you haven't been faithful with that wicked thing called money, who is going to entrust you with true wealth? [12]And if you haven't been faithful in looking after what belongs to someone else, who is going to give you what is your own?

[13]'Nobody can serve two masters. You will end up hating one and loving the other, or going along with the first and despising the other. You can't serve God and money.'

[14]The Pharisees, who loved money, heard all this, and mocked Jesus. [15]So he said to them, 'You people let everyone else know that you're in the right – but God knows your hearts. What people call honourable, God calls abominable!

[16]'The law and the prophets lasted until John. From now on, God's kingdom is announced, and everyone is trying to attack it. [17]But it's easier for heaven and earth to pass away than for one dot of an "i" to drop out of the law.'

Wealth is a killer. About half the stories in the newspapers seem to be about money in one way or another – the glamour and glitz it seems to provide, the shock and the horror when it runs out, the never-ending scandals about people getting it, embezzling it, losing it and getting it again. The lines between legitimate business and sharp practice are notoriously blurred. When does a gift become a bribe? When is it right to use other people's money to make money for yourself, and when is it wrong? And then there are the robberies, burglaries, and the numerous other obvious ways in which money is at the centre of simple, old-fashioned wrongdoing.

From a parable about money, Luke moves us to actual teaching about money. This passage contains some of Jesus' strongest and most explicit warnings about the dangers of wealth, and experience suggests that neither the church nor the world has taken these warnings sufficiently to heart. Somewhere along the line serious repentance, and a renewed determination to hear and obey Jesus' clear teaching, seems called for.

The key to it all is in the opening verses: it's about *faithfulness*. Money is not a possession, it's a trust: God entrusts property to people and expects it to be used to his glory and the welfare of his children, not for private glory or glamour. Money also, according to this passage, points beyond itself, to the true riches which await us in the life to come. What they are, we can hardly guess; but there are 'true riches' which really will belong to us, in a way that money doesn't, if we learn faithfulness here and now.

If we don't, we shall find ourselves torn between two masters. This situation was particularly acute in Jesus' day. As in most peasant societies, there was a very small number of extremely rich people and a very large number of the very poor. The rich included the chief priests (some of their opulent houses in Jerusalem have been discovered by archaeologists), so any attack on the rich would include an attack on them. The Pharisees were more of a populist movement; but the danger they faced, with the land as a key part of their religion, was that they would equate possession of land, and the wealth it brought, with God's blessing. Here Jesus makes it clear that this was not the way. He insists starkly that God's standards are not just subtly different from human ones, but are the exact opposite.

Is Jesus saying something new in all this? The Pharisees might well have answered him by pointing out that there was much in the Jewish law which encouraged people to think that possessions were a sign of God's favour. Jesus, of course, takes the opposite view, with a good deal of the prophetic writings obviously on his side; and the law itself commanded Israel to care for the poor and needy. His relationship to the Jewish law, though, is not exactly straightforward, and verses 16–17 need examining with some care.

He sees the law and the prophets (meaning the books we call 'the Old Testament') as taking their place in a sequence of events within God's plan. They are not God's last word; they hold sway until the time of John the Baptist, after which God's kingdom has been coming in a new way. Something fresh is happening here, where Jesus is; but this doesn't mean that the law and the prophets were wrong, or are now irrelevant. They remain fixed and unalterable. They are a true signpost to what God is going to do, even though they cannot themselves bring about the new day, the new world, that God is creating through Jesus. When, therefore, God does what he intends to do through Jesus, the law and the prophets will look on in approval, even though they couldn't have done it by themselves.

Putting the passage together, we find the underlying challenge to be faithful: faithful in our use of money, faithful to God rather than money, faithful in our hearts not just in our outward appearances.

For Reflection or Discussion

Do you ever think of money, or land, or other people, as commodities you're entitled to own or exploit? What would be a better, more faithful way to think of them?

WEEK 2: THURSDAY

The Parable of the Rich Man and Lazarus: Luke 16.19–31

[19]'There was once a rich man,' said Jesus, 'who was dressed in purple and fine linen, and feasted in splendour every day. [20]A poor man named Lazarus, who was covered with sores, lay outside his gate. [21]He longed to feed himself with the scraps that fell from the rich man's table. Even the dogs came and licked his sores.

[22]'In due course the poor man died, and was carried by the angels into Abraham's bosom. The rich man also died, and was buried. [23]As he was being tormented in Hades, he looked up and saw Abraham far away, and Lazarus in his bosom.

[24]'"Father Abraham!" he called out. "Have pity on me! Send Lazarus to dip the tip of his finger in water and cool my tongue! I'm in agony in this fire!"

[25]'"My child," replied Abraham, "remember that in your life you received good things, and in the same way Lazarus received evil. Now he is comforted here, and you are tormented. [26]Besides that, there is a great chasm standing between us. People who want to cross over from here to you can't do so, nor can anyone get across from the far side to us."

[27]'"Please, then, father," he said, "send him to my father's house. [28]I've got five brothers. Let him tell them about it, so that they don't come into this torture-chamber."

[29]'"They've got Moses and the prophets," replied Abraham. "Let them listen to them."

[30]'"No, father Abraham," he replied, "but if someone went to them from the dead, they would repent!"

[31]'"If they don't listen to Moses and the prophets," came the reply, "neither would they be convinced, even if someone rose from the dead."'

We have all seen him. He lies on a pile of newspapers outside a shop doorway, covered with a rough blanket. Perhaps he has a dog with him for safety. People walk past him, or even step over him. He occasionally rattles a few coins in a tin or cup, asking for more. He wasn't there when I was a boy, but he's there now, in all our cities, east, west, north and south.

As I see him, I hear voices. It's his own fault, they say. He's chosen it. There are agencies to help him. He should go and get a job. If we give him money he'll only spend it on drink. Stay away – he might be violent. Sometimes, in some places, the police will move him on, exporting the problem somewhere else. But he'll be back. And even if he isn't, there are whole societies like that. They camp in tin shacks on the edges of large, rich cities. From the doors of their tiny makeshift shelters you can see the high-rise hotels and office blocks where, if they're very lucky, one member of the family might work as a cleaner. They have been born into debt, and in debt they will stay, through the fault of someone rich and powerful who signed away their rights, their lives in effect, a generation or two ago, in return for arms, a new presidential palace, a fat Swiss bank account. And even if rich and poor don't always live side by side so blatantly, the television brings us together.

So we all know Lazarus. He is our neighbour. Some of us may be rich, well dressed and well fed, and walk past him without even noticing; others of us may not be so rich, or so finely clothed and fed, but compared with Lazarus we're well off. He would be glad to change places with us, and we would be horrified to share his life, even for a day.

Jesus' story about Lazarus and the unnamed rich man (he's often called 'Dives', because that's the Latin word for 'rich', but in the story he remains anonymous) works at several levels. It is very like a well-known folk tale in the ancient world; Jesus was by no means the first to tell of how wealth and poverty might be reversed in the future life. In fact, stories like this were so well known that we can see how Jesus has changed the pattern that people would expect. In the usual story, when someone asks permission to send a message back to the people who are still alive on earth, the permission is granted. Here, it isn't; and the sharp ending of the story points beyond itself to all sorts of questions that Jesus' hearers, and Luke's readers, were urged to face.

The parable is not primarily a moral tale about riches and poverty – though, in this chapter, it should be heard in that way as well. If that's all it was, some might say that it was better to let the poor stay poor, since they will have a good time in the future life. That sort of argument has been used too often by the careless rich for us to want anything to do with it. No; there is something more going on here. The story, after all, doesn't add anything new to the general folk belief about fortunes being reversed in a future life. But if it's a *parable*, that means we should take it as picture-language about something that was going on in Jesus' own work.

The ending gives us a clue: 'Neither would they be convinced, even if someone rose from the dead.' Jesus, we recall, has been criticized for welcoming outcasts and sinners; now it appears that what he's doing is putting into practice *in the present world* what, it was widely believed, would happen in the future one. 'On earth as it is in heaven' remains his watchword. The age to come must be anticipated in the present.

The point is then that the Pharisees, being themselves lovers of money, were behaving towards the people Jesus was welcoming exactly like the rich man was behaving towards Lazarus. And, just like the rich man, the Pharisees, and anyone else tempted to take a similar line, are now urged to change their ways while there is still time. All Jesus is asking them, in fact, is to do what Moses and the prophets would have said. As Luke makes clear throughout, his kingdom-mission is the fulfilment of the whole story of Israel. Anyone who understands the law and the prophets must therefore see that Jesus is bringing them to completion.

If they do not, then not even someone rising from the dead will bring them to their senses. The last sentence of the parable, like a great crashing chord on an organ, contains several different notes. It speaks of the whole hope of Israel for restoration and renewal. It speaks of the poor and outcast being welcomed by Jesus. And it speaks, for Luke's readers from that day to this, most powerfully of Jesus himself. One day soon, the reader knows, the law and the prophets will all come true in a new way, as Jesus himself rises again, opening the door to God's new age in which all wrongs will be put right.

For Reflection or Discussion

How, during his ministry, did Jesus anticipate the 'new age' promised by God in the law and the prophets? What should that mean for the church's ministry in the present?

WEEK 2: FRIDAY

The Rich Young Ruler: Luke 18.15–30

[15]People were bringing even tiny babies to Jesus for him to touch them. When the disciples saw it, they forbade them sternly. [16]But Jesus called them. 'Let the children come to me,' he said, 'and don't stop them! God's kingdom belongs to the likes of these. [17]I'm telling you the truth: anyone who doesn't receive God's kingdom like a child will never get into it.'

[18]There was a ruler who asked him, 'Good teacher, what must I do to inherit the life of the age to come?'

[19]'Why call me good?' said Jesus to him. 'No one is good except God alone. [20]You know the commandments: Don't commit adultery, don't kill, don't steal, don't swear falsely, honour your father and mother.'

[21]'I've kept them all', he said, 'since I was a boy.'

[22]When Jesus heard that, he said to him, 'There's just one thing you're short of. Sell everything you own, and distribute it to the poor, and you will have treasure in heaven. Then come and follow me.'

[23]When he heard that he turned very sad; he was extremely wealthy.

[24]Jesus saw that he had become sad, and said, 'How hard it is for those with possessions to enter God's kingdom! [25]Yes: it's easier for a camel to go through the eye of a needle than for a rich man to enter God's kingdom.'

[26]The people who heard it said, 'So who can be saved?'

[27]'What's impossible for humans', said Jesus, 'is possible for God.'

[28]'Look here,' said Peter, 'we've left everything and followed you.'

[29]'I'm telling you the truth,' said Jesus, 'everyone who has left house or wife or brothers or parents or children, because of God's kingdom, [30]will receive far more in return in the

48

> present time – and in the age to come they will receive the
> life that belongs to that age.'

Luke, ever the artist, is building up his great picture with
colour after colour, layer after layer of paint, until he draws
the eye towards the great scene he has in mind when Jesus
arrives in Jerusalem. He speaks here of the extraordinary
challenge of entering God's kingdom, of sharing the life of
the age to come.

Luke emphasizes how young the babies were that people
were bringing to Jesus. Jesus' rebuke to the disciples rings
out still today in a world where thousands of children are
treated as sub-human, as disposable commodities. These
are the ones, he says, who most truly show us what it means
to accept and enter God's kingdom. There is something
about the helplessness of children, and their complete
trust of those who love and care for them, which perfectly
demonstrates the humble trust he has been speaking of all
along. Jesus doesn't offer a romantic or sentimental view of
children; he must have known, in the daily life of a village,
and through growing up as the oldest of several children,
just how demanding and annoying they can be. But he sees
to the heart of what it means to receive God's kingdom; it is
like drinking in one's mother's milk, like learning to see –
and to smile! – by looking at one's mother's eyes and face.

By contrast, the rich ruler who appears so confident,
so well organized, so determined, looks into the face of
the one he calls 'good' and turns away sad. He had hoped
to impress Jesus with his piety and devotion; unlike the
'sinners' of whom we have heard so much in the previous chapters, he had a clean moral record in keeping the
well-known commandments. His question, Jesus' answer,

and the subsequent conversation with the crowd and the disciples, enable us to see to the heart of what is going on as Jesus approaches Jerusalem.

Jesus was putting into operation that for which most Jews had longed: God's kingdom, God's sovereign saving power operating in a new way for the benefit of the whole world. This meant that already, in the present, the period of time they spoke of as 'the age to come' was breaking in. It would come fully in the future, when all evil had been done away with, and then those who belonged to it would share 'the life of the coming age'. Because the word for 'age' here is often translated 'eternal', the phrase 'eternal life' has regularly been used to describe this life. For many today, this simply means an existence going on and on for ever. This may or may not be desirable; opinions will differ. But in any case it doesn't catch the flavour, the sheer excitement, carried by the original.

In God's new age, so the Jews believed, everything will be new, fresh, and free from corruption, decay, evil, bitterness, pain, fear and death. And that's just the beginning. There will be new possibilities and opportunities, new joys and delights. Heaven and earth will be joined together, God and his children will live with each other. That's the state of things people were longing for. It would come about when God finally ruled the world with his saving power.

And this is what Jesus was bringing in the present. Evil and death, to be sure, were still going on all around. Jesus himself had yet to face the full force of the powers of the old age. But where he was, and where people with humble and penitent trust accepted that God's kingdom was active in and through him, there the life of the new age began to be seen.

That was why the rich ruler became sad. In order to inherit the life of the new age, he had to abandon the values of the old and trust himself totally to the new, like a diver throwing himself forwards into the water. He couldn't seriously be seeking for the new age if he couldn't abandon the symbols of the old. The commandments were good and important; but if he was wedded to possessions then he would never be able to accept God's kingdom like a child, with the humble trust that allowed God to be God. The true wealth is to be found in the heavenly dimension: 'treasure in heaven' doesn't simply mean the sort of treasure you possess after you die, but treasure that's kept safe in God's storehouse until the time when heaven and earth are brought into their intended unity.

Already, even in the present time, this new age breaks in to our sad old world. Within the life of Christian fellowship there are new homes, new families, new possibilities that open up for those who leave behind the old ways. The church is called in every age to be that sort of community, a living example of the age to come. In that sort of selfless and trusting common life church members themselves, and the world around, can glimpse what God's new world is like, and learn to live that way more and more.

For Reflection or Discussion

In what ways are you or your church a living example of the age to come? What elements of the old age might you need to abandon and let go of if you're going to live more fully the life of the kingdom to which you've been called?

WEEK 2: SATURDAY

The Calling of Zacchaeus: Luke 19.1–10

[1]They went into Jericho and passed through. [2]There was a man named Zacchaeus, a chief tax-collector, who was very rich. [3]He was trying to see who Jesus was, but, being a small man, he couldn't, because of the crowd. [4]So he ran on ahead, along the route Jesus was going to take, and climbed up into a sycamore tree to see him.

[5]When Jesus came to the place, he looked up.

'Zacchaeus,' he said to him, 'hurry up and come down. I have to stay at your house today.' So he hurried up, came down, and welcomed him with joy.

[7]Everybody began to murmur when they saw it. 'He's gone in to spend time with a proper old sinner!' they were saying.

[8]But Zacchaeus stood there and addressed the master.

'Look, Master,' he said, 'I'm giving half my property to the poor. And if I have defrauded anyone of anything, I'm giving it back to them four times over.'

[9]'Today,' said Jesus, 'salvation has come to this house, because he too is a son of Abraham. [10]You see, the son of man came to seek and to save the lost.'

Sunday schools love Zacchaeus. At least, they love to act out his story and sing about him. The little man who climbs up a tree to see Jesus provides one of the most vivid short stories in the whole Bible. Children can identify with Zacchaeus; they often find themselves at the back of a crowd and can't see what's going on. Many adults, too, can identify with him; they might like to get closer to Jesus, but find it embarrassing to do so, and potentially costly.

Luke, of course, makes Zacchaeus one of his minor heroes. Luke's is the only gospel that tells of him and his sudden moment of glory, and the hardened old tax-collector fits in to three of Luke's regular themes: the problem of riches and what to do about it, the identification of Jesus with 'sinners', and the faith which recognizes Jesus as Lord and discovers new life as a result. This kind of healing, this kind of new life, he seems to be saying, is what Jesus has come to bring. If only people in Jerusalem could see the point and make a similar response!

Nobody in Jericho liked Zacchaeus. They would have been horrified to think that, of all the inhabitants of the town, he would be the one known by name to millions of people 2,000 years later. He was exactly the kind of man everybody despised. Not only a tax-collector but a chief tax-collector; that is, not only did he make money on the side, in addition to his legitimate collections, but he almost certainly made more money from the tax-collectors working under him. Wherever money changes hands, whether across a grubby table in a tin shack in a dusty small town or across a sparkling computer screen in a shiny office on the ninety-ninth floor of a Wall Street skyscraper, the hands all too easily get dirty. Whenever money starts to talk, it shouts louder than the claims of honesty, respect and human dignity. One can only imagine the reaction of neighbours, and even of friends and relatives, as Zacchaeus's house became more lavishly decorated, as more slaves ran about at his bidding, as his clothes became finer and his food richer. Everyone knew that this was their money and that he had no right to it; everyone knew that there was nothing they could do about it.

Until Jesus came through the town. The moment when the eyes of the two men met is worthy of an operatic aria. Inquisitiveness had got the better of the little rich man, an unspoken question emerging from behind his hard, crafty look. Jesus saw straight through the layers of graft and greed, of callous contempt for his fellow citizens. He had met enough tax-collectors already to know exactly what life was like for them, and how, even though they couldn't resist the chance to make more for themselves than they should, there was a sickness at the heart for which he had the remedy.

So once again Jesus finds himself relaxing in the company of the wrong sort of people. And once again the crowd outside grumble. But this time, instead of Jesus telling a parable, the tax-collector himself speaks to Jesus in public, and gives evidence of his extravagant repentance. Repentance here isn't just a change of heart; as in Judaism in general, repentance involves restoration and renewal, making amends. Zacchaeus is determined to do so lavishly. He doesn't offer to sell all his property, nor does Jesus demand it. But by the time he'd given half of it away, and made fourfold restitution where necessary, we can imagine that he would find himself in seriously reduced circumstances.

He doesn't care. He has found something more valuable. 'Today I have to stay at your house' becomes 'Today salvation has come to this house'; where Jesus is, there salvation is to be found, for those who accept him as master and reorder their lives accordingly. Once more Jesus links a former outcast back into the true family of Abraham (compare 13.16). Zacchaeus isn't going to follow Jesus on the road to Jerusalem, escaping the puzzled and probably still angry looks of the neighbours. He is going to live out his new life and re-establish himself as part of the renewed Israel right where he is.

For Reflection or Discussion

Why does genuine and lasting renewal depend on repentance, restoration and tangible changes to the way someone thinks and lives?

WEEK 3: A TIME FOR JUSTICE

THIRD SUNDAY OF ADVENT

John the Baptist Confronts the Crowds: Luke 3.7–18

[7]'You brood of vipers,' John used to say to the crowds who came out to be baptized by him. 'Who told you to escape from the coming anger? [8]You'd better prove your repentance by bearing the proper fruit! Don't start saying to yourselves, "We have Abraham as our father"; let me tell you, God can raise up children for Abraham from these stones! [9]The axe is already standing by the roots of the tree – so every tree that doesn't produce good fruit will be cut down and thrown into the fire.'

[10]'What shall we do?' asked the crowds.

[11]'Anyone who has two cloaks', replied John, 'should give one to someone who hasn't got one. The same applies to anyone who has plenty of food.'

[12]Some toll-collectors came to be baptized. 'Teacher,' they said, 'what should we do?'

[13]'Don't collect more than what is laid down,' he replied.

[14]Some soldiers, too, asked John, 'What about us? What should we do?'

'No extortion,' replied John, 'and no blackmail. Be content with your wages.'

[15]The people were very excited, and everyone was questioning in their hearts whether John might not be the Messiah. [16]To all of them, John responded: 'I am baptizing you with water. But someone is coming who is stronger than I am. I don't deserve to untie his sandal-strap. He will baptize you with the holy spirit and with fire. [17]He will have his winnowing-fork to hand, ready to sort out the mess on his threshing floor and gather the corn into his

barn. Any rubbish he will burn with a fire that will never go out.'

¹⁸John urged his news on the people with many other words.

A cartoon shows a sceptic shouting up to the heavens, 'God! If you're up there, tell us what we should do!'

Back comes a voice: 'Feed the hungry, house the homeless, establish justice.'

The sceptic looks alarmed. 'Just testing,' he says.

'Me too,' replies the voice.

John the Baptist doesn't seem to have wasted time and breath going into the details of ethical debate. Not for him the learned discussions of particular cases, the small details of law that take time and energy away from actually doing anything about the way the world is – and the way one's own life is. Of course, one might grumble that John hadn't said anything to the people who *didn't* have two cloaks or too much food, but that wasn't the point. If people were coming for baptism, they were committing themselves to be God's Israel, the light of the world, the people in whom God's justice would be seen by all. There was no time, and no need, for lengthy discussions such as we find in the writings of the rabbis. What they needed were rules of thumb. 'Two cloaks? Give one away. Too much food? Same applies.' Nobody could miss the point. Like the great Old Testament prophets, John could see the rich getting richer and the poor poorer. A start had to be made to get things back on track.

The special cases are doubly interesting. Nobody likes paying taxes at the best of times, and some of the tolls were levied simply at the whim of local rulers, shamelessly lining their pockets and giving the collectors tacit licence to do the same. John doesn't say they should stop working for the hated rulers; he's not going to recommend unemployment. But they must earn their living and no more. No getting rich at the expense of their own people.

The soldiers are probably from Herod's own troops; they are unlikely to be Roman soldiers, coming to a Jewish prophet for a ritual that only made sense within Israel's national story. Like the toll-collectors, they aren't told to abandon their careers, but they must avoid abusing their position, as was evidently commonplace. No thuggery, using their brute force to rob people with impunity. 'Be content with your wages' isn't a way of telling them not to campaign for higher wages from their employers; the steady creeping inflation that modern Western economies experience was virtually unknown in the first-century Roman world, and annual pay rises would not have been an issue. Rather, the soldiers are not to use a complaint about low pay as an excuse to rob and pillage ('Herod doesn't pay us enough, so we have no choice').

Simple, clear commands; but if they were obeyed they would demonstrate that people meant business. None of these things happens by chance; they only occur when people have genuinely repented of the small-scale injustices which turn a society sour. But there is more. John is not just a moral reformer; he is the herald of the Messiah.

Jesus himself would give more detailed teaching than John. But he never retreated from the things John was saying here. He too was just as committed as John to God's justice working its way out into the world in the behaviour of his followers. For him, God's justice would be displayed not through riches and royalty of worldly style, but through the love and justice that would finally be combined on the cross.

For Reflection or Discussion

Can you think of examples of injustices – whether large-scale or small-scale – that have been reported in the news recently? What do you imagine John the Baptist would say about them were he alive today?

WEEK 3: MONDAY

Opposition to Jesus in Nazareth: Luke 4.14–30

[14]Jesus returned to Galilee in the power of the spirit. Word about him went out throughout the whole district. [15]He taught in their synagogues, and gained a great reputation all around.

[16]He came to Nazareth, where he had been brought up. On the Sabbath, as was his regular practice, he went into the synagogue and stood up to read. [17]They gave him the scroll of the prophet Isaiah. He unrolled the scroll and found the place where it was written:

[18]The spirit of the Lord is upon me
because he has anointed me
to tell the poor the good news.
He has sent me to announce release to the prisoners
and sight to the blind,
to set the wounded victims free,
[19]to announce the year of God's special favour.

[20]He rolled up the scroll, gave it to the attendant, and sat down. All eyes in the synagogue were fixed on him.

²¹'Today,' he began, 'this scripture is fulfilled in your own hearing.'

²²Everyone remarked at him; they were astonished at the words coming out of his mouth – words of sheer grace.

'Isn't this Joseph's son?' they said.

²³'I know what you're going to say,' Jesus said. 'You're going to tell me the old riddle: "Heal yourself, doctor!" "We heard of great happenings in Capernaum; do things like that here, in your own country!"

²⁴'Let me tell you the truth,' he went on. 'Prophets never get accepted in their own country. ²⁵This is the solemn truth: there were plenty of widows in Israel in the time of Elijah, when heaven was shut up for three years and six months, and there was a great famine over all the land. ²⁶Elijah was sent to none of them, only to a widow in the Sidonian town of Zarephath.

²⁷'And there were plenty of people with virulent skin diseases in Israel in the time of Elisha the prophet, and none of them was healed – only Naaman, the Syrian.'

²⁸When they heard this, everyone in the synagogue flew into a rage. ²⁹They got up and threw him out of town. They took him to the top of the mountain on which the town was built, meaning to fling him off. ³⁰But he slipped through the middle of them and went away.

The commentators were ecstatic after the game. 'He played like a man inspired,' they said. What images does that conjure up for you?

A sports star, perhaps, running rings round the opposition and scoring a brilliant goal.

Or, from a different world, a musician: eyes closed, fingers flying to and fro on an instrument, filling the air with wonderful jazz.

'Inspiration': we use the word loosely. We imply that 'it just came over them', that they suddenly became someone different. Of course we know that it didn't happen like that. The brilliant athlete has been training and practising, hour after hour and week after week. The musician has been playing exercises, perfecting technique for long hours out of the public eye. Then, when the moment comes, a surge of adrenalin produces a performance which we call 'inspired' – but which is actually the fruit of long, patient hard work.

When Jesus said 'the spirit of the Lord is upon me', Luke has already let us into the secret. His years of silent preparation. His life of prayer leading up to his baptism. The confirmation of his vocation – and then its testing in the wilderness. Then, at last, going public with early deeds in Capernaum (as the exchange in the Nazareth synagogue makes clear, people had already heard of what he'd done elsewhere). Now, with years of prayer, thought and the study of scripture behind him, he stands before his own town. He knew everybody there and they knew him. He preached like a man inspired; indeed, in his sermon that's what he claimed. But what he said was the opposite of what they were expecting. If this was inspiration, they didn't want it.

What was so wrong with what he said? What made them kick him out of the synagogue, hustle him out of the town, and take him off to the cliff edge to throw him over?

The crucial part comes in Jesus' comments to his hearers. He senses that they aren't following him; they are ready to taunt him with proverbs, to challenge him to do some mighty deeds for the sake of show. 'Heal yourself, doctor!' – the challenge is not too far removed from the taunt, 'He saved others, but he can't save himself' (23.35). But why? What was so wrong with what he was saying?

By way of defence and explanation for the line he had been taking, Jesus points out what happened in the days of the great prophets Elijah and Elisha, and in doing so identifies himself with the prophets. Elijah was sent to help a widow – but not a Jewish one. Elisha healed one solitary leper – and the leper was the commander of the enemy army. That's what did it. That's what drove them to fury. Israel's God was rescuing the wrong people.

The earlier part of Jesus' address must have been hammering home the same point. His hearers were, after all, waiting for God to liberate Israel from pagan enemies. In several Jewish texts of the time, we find a longing that God would condemn the wicked nations, would pour out wrath and destruction on them. Instead, Jesus is pointing out that when the great prophets were active, it wasn't Israel who benefited, but the pagans. That's like someone in Britain or France during the Second World War speaking of God's healing and restoration for Adolf Hitler. It's not what people wanted to hear.

What, then, was the earlier part of his address about?

Luke says that the people 'were astonished at the words of sheer grace that were coming out of his mouth'. Sometimes people have understood this simply to mean, 'they were astonished at what a good speaker he was'. But it seems more likely that he means 'they were astonished that he was speaking about God's grace – grace for everybody, including the nations – instead of grace for Israel and fierce judgment for everyone else'. That fits perfectly with what followed.

Why then did Jesus begin his address with the long quotation from Isaiah (61.1–2)?

The passage he quotes is about the Messiah. Throughout Isaiah there are pictures of a strange 'anointed' figure who will perform the Lord's will and execute God's justice. But, though this text goes on to speak of vengeance on evildoers, Jesus doesn't quote that bit. Instead, he seems to have drawn on the larger picture in Isaiah and elsewhere which speaks of Israel being called to be the light of the nations, a theme which Luke has already highlighted in chapter 2. The servant-Messiah has not come to inflict punishment on the nations, but to bring God's love and mercy to them. And that will be the fulfilment of a central theme in Israel's own scriptures.

This message was, and remains, shocking. Jesus' claim to be reaching out with healing to all people, though itself a vital Jewish idea, was not what most first-century Jews wanted or expected. As we shall see, Jesus coupled it with severe warnings to his own countrymen. Unless they could see that this was the time for their God to be gracious, unless they abandoned their futile dreams of a military victory over their national enemies, they would suffer defeat themselves at every level – military, political and theological.

Here, as at the climax of the gospel story, Jesus' challenge and warning brings about a violent reaction. The gospel still does this today, when it challenges all interests and agendas, all forms of injustice and oppression, with the news of God's surprising grace.

For Reflection or Discussion

How does God's grace challenge human interests and agendas, and what sorts of interests and agendas – whether military, political or theological – are causing or perpetuating forms of injustice in the wold today?

WEEK 3: TUESDAY

Jesus Sends Out the Seventy: Luke 10.1–16

[1]After this the master commissioned seventy others, and sent them ahead of him in pairs to every town and place where he was intending to come.

[2]'There's a great harvest out there,' he said to them, 'but there aren't many workers. So plead with the harvest-master to send out workers for the harvest.

[3]'Off you go now. Remember, I'm sending you out like lambs among wolves. [4]Take no money-bag, no pack, no sandals – and don't stop to pass the time with anyone on the road. [5]Whenever you go into a house, first say, "Peace on this house." [6]If a child of peace lives there, your peace will rest on them; but if not, it will return to you.

[7]'Stay in the same house, and eat and drink what they provide. The worker deserves to be paid, you see. Don't go from house to house. [8]If you go into a town and they welcome you, eat what is provided, [9]heal the sick who are there, and say to them, "God's kingdom has come close to you." [10]But if you go into a town and they don't welcome you, go out into the streets of the town and say, [11]"Here is the very dust of your town clinging to our feet – and we're wiping it off in front of your eyes! [12]But you should know this: God's kingdom has come close to you!" Let me tell you, on that day it will be more tolerable for Sodom than for that town.

¹³'Woe betide you, Chorazin! Woe betide you, Bethsaida! If the powerful deeds done in you had been done in Tyre and Sidon, they would have repented long ago, sitting in sackcloth and ashes. ¹⁴But it will be more tolerable for Tyre and Sidon in the judgment than for you. ¹⁵And you, Capernaum – you want to be lifted up to heaven, do you? No: you'll be sent down to Hades!

¹⁶'Anyone who hears you, hears me; anyone who rejects you, rejects me; and anyone who rejects me, rejects the one who sent me.'

I had lunch with a friend who told me how, earlier in the year, his teenage son had been taken seriously ill. For weeks he had been going to doctors and specialists, all of whom had been puzzled by his symptoms. Finally he went to a senior specialist, who put an end to the speculation. 'Take him to the hospital at once,' he said. 'We'll operate tomorrow.' He had discovered a brain tumour, which was removed with great skill and without lasting damage. Had they waited another day it might have been too late.

Something of that mood hangs over the story of Jesus' second sending out of followers. This time, when Jesus sends messengers to the places he intends to visit, there is a note of real urgency. He knows he will not pass this way again; if people don't respond to his mission this time, it may be too late. He is the last herald before the great debacle that will come on the nation if they don't pay attention. If they reject him, there can be no subsequent warning. If they delay, it may be too late.

Only Luke tells us of a mission of seventy, and there are two puzzles about this. First, some manuscripts read 'seventy-two', instead of 'seventy', and there has been much discussion about which is correct. Second, whichever it is, why was this number chosen (either by Jesus or Luke)? Was there a symbolic meaning for it?

The answer to both questions may be that once again Luke is seeing Jesus in the light of Moses, who on one occasion chose seventy elders of Israel, who were given a share in God's spirit, and were thereby equipped to help him lead the people of Israel (Numbers 11.16, 25). On that occasion two others who were not part of the original seventy also received the spirit, to the alarm of some. The point will then be that Jesus is sending out assistants to help in leading the new exodus.

But in the original exodus the Israelites rebelled, grumbled and didn't want to go the way God was leading. That, indeed, was the main reason why Moses needed extra help. In Jesus' work, too, many if not most of his contemporaries simply didn't want to know. Despite all his healings, and the power and shrewdness of his teaching, the way he wanted them to follow – the way which he knew would lead them to God's true exodus – was simply not the way they wanted. Thus it had been since his first sermon at Nazareth; thus it was to be right up to his last days in Jerusalem.

At the heart of his call was the message of peace. 'Peace to this house,' the messengers were to say, looking to see whether there was a 'child of peace' there. Jesus' contemporaries were for the most part not wanting peace – peace with their traditional enemies the Samaritans, or peace with the feared and hated Romans. They wanted an all-out war that would bring God's justice swiftly to their aid and get rid of their enemies once and for all.

But Jesus' vision of God's kingdom, and of God's just-ice, was going in the opposite direction. As far as he was concerned, the idea of fighting evil with evil was like the children of Israel wanting to go back to Egypt. Other movements had tried the way of violence, with disastrous results. But his rejection of that way was not based simply on pragmatic considerations. It grew directly out of his knowledge and love of Israel's God as the God of generous grace and astonishing, powerful, healing love. This was the God whose life-giving power flowed through him to heal; this was the God to whose kingdom he was committed.

His messengers therefore had to go with a word of warn-ing as well as of invitation. To refuse this message would mean courting the disaster of going the opposite way from God himself; and that would mean, as always, throwing oneself into the hands of pagan power. The judgment that would fall on Chorazin and Bethsaida in central Galilee, and on Jesus' own town of Capernaum, would be more terrible than that suffered by the wicked cities of the Old Testament, but it would not consist of fire falling from heaven. It would take the form of Roman invasion and destruction. Rome's punishment for rebel subjects would be the direct result of God's people turning away from God's way of peace.

This explains the urgency and sternness of Jesus' charge to the seventy. They were not offering people a new reli-gious option which might have a gentle effect on their lives. They were holding out the last chance for people to turn away from Israel's flight into ruin, and to accept God's way of peace. God's kingdom – God's sovereign and saving rule, longing to enfold his people and the whole world with love and new creation – had come close to them. Jesus was on his way to Jerusalem for the showdown with the forces of evil and injustice. To reject him now, or even to reject his messengers, was to reject God himself.

For Reflection or Discussion

How did Jesus' vision of God's justice and peace differ from that of most of his contemporaries? Why was he against fighting evil with evil?

WEEK 3: WEDNESDAY

Woes against the Pharisees: Luke 11.42–54

[42]'But woe betide you Pharisees!' Jesus continued. 'You tithe mint and rue and herbs of all kinds; and you have side-stepped justice, mercy and the love of God. You should have done these, without missing out the others.

[43]'Woe betide you Pharisees! You love the chief seats in the synagogues and greetings in the market-places.

[44]'Woe betide you! You are like hidden tombs, and people walk over them without knowing it.'

[45]At this, one of the legal experts spoke up. 'Teacher,' he said, 'when you say this you're insulting us too!'

[46]'Woe betide you lawyers, too!' replied Jesus. 'You give people heavy loads to carry which they can hardly bear, and you yourselves don't lift a finger to help.

[47]'Woe betide you! You build the tombs of the prophets, and your ancestors killed them. [48]So you bear witness that you approve of what your ancestors did: they killed them, and you build their tombs.

[49]'For all this, God's Wisdom says, "I'm sending you prophets and ambassadors; some of them you will kill and

68

persecute", [50]so that the blood of all the prophets shed ever since the beginning of the world may be required from this generation – [51]from the blood of Abel to the blood of Zacharias, who died between the altar and the sanctuary. Yes, let me tell you, it will all be required from this generation.

[52]'Woe betide you lawyers! You have taken away the key of knowledge. You didn't go in yourselves, and you stopped the people who were trying to go in.'

[53]He went outside, and the scribes and Pharisees began to be very threatening towards him. They interrogated him about several things, [54]lying in wait for him to catch him in something he might say.

The tennis player came grumpily into the television interview room. He had just lost a vital match in the Wimbledon men's singles tournament, the premier tennis event of the year. He was tired and cross. Worse: in the course of the game, screened on live television, he had lost his temper and sworn at the umpire. It had not been a good day.

The interviewer was more interested in the swearing than in the tennis. Wasn't he sorry now, he asked, for what he had said?

The tennis player rounded on him.

'Are you perfect?' he demanded.

There was a confused splutter from the (unseen) interviewer, caught between the outrageous claim to perfection and the unthinkable admission that he, too, was human.

'Then shut up!' retorted the player, having made his point.

The incident itself became briefly more important than the tennis. The player had broken a law which, although unwritten, had been assumed by many in the media. *He had been rude to a journalist.*

Who are the Pharisees in today's society? Who are the lawyers who load heavy burdens on to people's backs but don't themselves lift a finger to shift them? When I was younger, passages like this used to be applied to religious teachers. Some people, we were told, insist on all kinds of religious observances. You should fast on Fridays, you should kneel down and stand up at the right points in church, you should cross yourself. You should earn as many celestial good marks as you could. Or, perhaps, you shouldn't play cards, you shouldn't wear make-up, you shouldn't go to the theatre. You should read your Bible every day. Either way, we were told, people who taught such things tried to make you focus on the things you did, rather than calling you simply to believe and trust God for your salvation.

Well, that sort of teacher does sometimes look like a kind of modern Pharisee. But there are two problems with that as the interpretation. First, the real Pharisees – the flesh-and-blood first-century Jewish Pharisees – weren't in fact very much like that at all. They held what we would call a strong *political* belief, backed up with religious sanctions: their rules were designed to make people keep the Jewish law as best they could, so that Israel would be made holy, and thus God would bring in the kingdom. The lawyers weren't trying to set up complex systems as hoops for people to jump through to make sure they were saved; they were trying to codify as much of the Jewish law as they could, working out more and more complex possibilities of situations that might arise when one would need to know what was the right thing to do. Neither

70

of these corresponds very closely to forms of Christian teaching, even degenerate forms, in the modern world.

Second, the Pharisees were a pressure group in what we would call the social and political sphere. They were far more like a group in society who take it upon themselves to urge people to obey particular codes: like those, for instance, who insist upon various 'green' policies for the disposal of rubbish. We may agree with the policies, but the point is that these aren't simply 'religious' duties in the old sense. And in particular, at least in the Western world where the press is relatively free, there are many whole newspapers, as well as individual journalists, who take it upon themselves to be the guardians of public morality. They will shriek in mock-horror at all kinds of offences, and take delight in pointing the finger at the rich and respectable. But at the same time many of the journalists who make a living by doing all this are by no means shining examples of moral virtue. In some cases they are the ones who load heavy burdens on people's backs but don't themselves lift a finger to move them.

Now clearly this only goes a little way towards explaining what's going on in this passage, but it's important to loosen ourselves up, away from an older interpretation that sees the Pharisees as simply 'religious leaders' in the sense we mean it today, and so to get out of our minds any idea that Jesus' solemn denunciation of them was simply what we might call 'religious polemic'. Jesus saw very clearly that there were many self-appointed teachers in the world of first-century Judaism who were using their learning partly for their own status and partly for their own political ends. And he, for whom learning and devotion were matters of love for God and for all people (as the best of the Pharisees would have agreed), saw that there was a choice facing the Israel of his day.

It wasn't a matter of *either* following millions of petty rules *or* of a pure, uncluttered religion of love and grace. It was a matter of an agenda which focused on the law as the charter of Israel's national life, on the one hand, and an agenda which demanded repentance, turning away from Israel's headlong flight into national rebellion, politically against Rome and theologically against God. There could be no compromise.

When Jesus announced these quite formal 'Woes', then, he wasn't simply saying he *disliked* such attitudes – the detailed outward observance that left the heart untouched, the piety that boosted self-importance, the pollution that appeared as clean and wholesome. It wasn't simply that he happened to disapprove of the objectionable practices of these other groups. It was, rather, that he could see where they would lead: to a terrible conflagration in which the present generation would pull down on its own head the pent-up devastation of the centuries.

'Scribes' refers literally to people trained in writing legal documents; it overlaps quite closely with 'lawyers'. They believed that Israel's law, the Torah, should be applied to every area of life, and so combined in themselves the modern roles of 'lawyer' and 'religious teacher', and much besides. It is small wonder that such people took offence at what Jesus was saying. If he was right, their entire programme was based on a huge mistake. If they were right, the mistake was his. The fierce opposition between them continues on and off right through to the final showdown in Jerusalem. For Luke, continuing the story of Jesus' journey towards his coming death, the warnings to the cities

(10.13–15), the battles with the demons at several points, and the controversies with these opponents, all form part of Jesus' profile. Jesus is not simply going to Jerusalem to teach. He is going there to bring to its head his whole message of God's justice and peace: a message which cut across much that passed for traditional teaching, a message which could not but prove fiercely controversial.

For Reflection or Discussion

What are the unjust and oppressive human agendas that the gospel of Jesus confronts in the world today? How can Christians be more effective in naming and combatting them?

WEEK 3: THURSDAY

The Parables of the Persistent Widow and the Tax-Collector: Luke 18.1–14

[1]Jesus told them a parable, about how they should always pray and not give up.

[2]'There was once a judge in a certain town,' he said, 'who didn't fear God, and didn't have any respect for people. [3]There was a widow in that town, and she came to him and said, "Judge my case! Vindicate me against my enemy!"

[4]'For a long time he refused. But, in the end, he said to himself, "It's true that I don't fear God, and don't have any respect for people. [5]But because this widow is causing me a lot of trouble, I will put her case right and vindicate her, so that she doesn't end up coming and giving me a black eye."

[6]'Well,' said the master, 'did you hear what this unjust judge says? [7]And don't you think that God will see justice done for his chosen ones, who shout out to him day and night?

Do you suppose he is deliberately delaying? [8]Let me tell you, he will vindicate them very quickly. But – when the son of man comes, will he find faith on the earth?'

[9]He told this next parable against those who trusted in their own righteous standing and despised others.

[10]'Two men', he said, 'went up to the Temple to pray. One was a Pharisee, the other was a tax-collector. [11]The Pharisee stood and prayed in this way to himself: "God, I thank you that I am not like the other people – greedy, unjust, immoral, or even like this tax-collector. [12]I fast twice in the week; I give tithes of all that I get."

[13]'But the tax-collector stood a long way off, and didn't even want to raise his eyes to heaven. He beat his breast and said, "God, be merciful to me, sinner that I am." [14]Let me tell you, he was the one who went back to his house vindicated by God, not the other. Don't you see? People who exalt themselves will be humbled, and people who humble themselves will be exalted.'

Come with me into a court of law, where a civil case is being tried. I haven't often been in a court, but we see them on the television and in the newspapers, and from time to time legal cases are widely reported and make history.

If it wasn't so serious, it would be like a sporting contest. Here is the plaintiff, claiming eagerly that he has been wronged by the person opposing him. He has his team of lawyers, and they are arguing the case, producing witnesses, trying to persuade the judge that he is in the right. Here, opposite, is the defendant, the man the plaintiff is accusing. He and his team are trying to persuade the judge that *he* is in the right. Though experts who are watching may have a sense of which way the verdict is going to go, the result isn't known until the judge, like a referee, finally sums up and announces the result.

In the ancient Jewish lawcourt, all cases were like that, not just civil ones. If someone had stolen from you, you had to bring a charge against them; you couldn't get the police to do it for you. If someone had murdered a relative of yours, the same would be true. So every legal case in Jesus' day was a matter of a judge deciding to vindicate one party or the other: 'vindication' or 'justification' here means upholding their side of the story, deciding in their favour. This word 'justification', which we meet a lot in Paul but hardly ever in the gospels, means exactly this: that the judge finds in one's favour at the end of the case. (See, e.g., Romans 2.1–16; 3.21–31; Galatians 2.16–21.)

These two parables, very different though they are in some ways, are both about vindication. The first is more obviously so, since it is actually set in a lawcourt; but here we are puzzled at first glance, since, though Jesus clearly intends the judge to stand for God, this judge is about as unlike God as possible. He has no respect for God himself, and he doesn't care whether he does the right thing for people or not. The point of the parable is then to say: if even a rotten judge like that can be persuaded to do the right thing by someone who pesters him day and night until it happens, then of course God, who is Justice in person, and who cares passionately about people, will vindicate them, will see that justice is done.

The parable assumes that God's people are like litigants in a lawsuit, waiting for God's verdict. What is the lawsuit about? It seems to be about Israel, or rather now the renewed Israel gathered around Jesus, awaiting from God the vindication that will come when those who have opposed his message are finally routed. It is, in other words, about the same scenario as described in the previous chapter: the time when, through the final destruction of the city and Temple that have opposed him, Jesus' followers will know that God has vindicated Jesus himself, and them as his followers. Though this moment will itself be terrifying, it will function as the liberating, vindicating judgment that God's people have been waiting and praying for. And if this is true of that final moment, it is also true of all such lesser moments, with which Christian living is filled.

The second parable looks at first as though it is describing a religious occasion, but it too turns out to be another lawsuit. Or perhaps we should say that the Pharisee in the Temple has already turned it into a contest: his 'prayer', which consists simply of telling God all about his own good points, ends up exalting himself by the simple expedient of denouncing the tax-collector. The tax-collector, however, is the one whose small faith sees through to the great heart of God (see 17.6), and he casts himself on the divine mercy. Jesus reveals what the divine judge would say about this: the tax-collector, not the Pharisee, returned home vindicated.

These two parables together make a powerful statement about what, in Paul's language, is called 'justification by faith'. The wider context is the final lawcourt, in which God's chosen people will be vindicated after their life of suffering, holiness and service. Though enemies outside and inside may denounce and attack them, God will act and show that they truly are his people. But this doesn't mean that one can tell in the present who God's elect are, simply by the outward badges of virtue, and in particular the observance of the minutiae of the Jewish law. If you want to see where this final vindication is anticipated in the present, look for where there is genuine penitence, genuine casting of oneself on the mercies of God. 'This one went home vindicated'; those are among the most comforting and encouraging words in the whole gospel.

For Reflection or Discussion

Is a desire for vindication the same as a desire for justice? How and in what circumstances do they differ?

WEEK 3: FRIDAY

The Parable of the Tenants: Luke 20.9–19

[9]Jesus began to tell the people this parable. 'There was a man who planted a vineyard, let it out to tenant farmers, and went abroad for a long while. [10]When the time came, he sent a slave to the farmers to collect from them some of the produce of the vineyard. But the farmers beat him and sent him away empty-handed. [11]He then sent a further slave, and they beat him, abused him, and sent him back empty-handed. [12]Then he sent yet a third, and they beat him up and threw him out.

[13]'So the master of the vineyard said, "What shall I do? I'll send my beloved son. They will certainly respect him!" [14]But when the farmers saw him they said to each other, "This is the heir! Let's kill him, and then the inheritance will belong to us!" [15]And they threw him out of the vineyard and killed him.

'So what will the master of the vineyard do? [16]He will come and wipe out those farmers, and give the vineyard to others.'

When they heard this, they said, 'God forbid!' [17]But Jesus looked round at them and said, 'What then does it mean in the Bible when it says,

The very stone the builders refused
Now for the corner's top is used?

[18]'Everyone who falls on that stone will be smashed to smithereens; but if it falls on anyone, it will crush them.'

[19]The scribes and the chief priests tried to lay hands on him then and there. But they were afraid of the people, because they knew that Jesus had told this parable against them.

One of the most dramatic scenes ever to take place in the British House of Commons occurred in January 1642. King Charles I went in person to the House to try to arrest five Members of Parliament who had opposed him. The Speaker of the House himself stood in his way, and prevented the king coming any further into the chamber where the Commons met. A painting of the incident hangs in the lobby of the Palace of Westminster to this day. It was something of a turning-point: another step on the road to civil war, and to the king's eventual execution.

No self-respecting first-century monarch would ever have allowed himself to get in that position; and no landowner would tolerate for very long the kind of behaviour described in this parable. But there are striking parallels between this story and the one Jesus told, his last explanation (in parable form) of what was going on in his coming to Jerusalem. The vineyard owner has sent messengers to the tenant farmers, to no effect. (No first-century Jew would have needed to be told that the owner stood for God, the farmers for Israel, and the messengers for the

78

prophets.) Finally, having no one left to send, he sent his own beloved son. In Jesus' own understanding, he came as the rightful king to his father's tenants; and they were barring his way, determined to keep the vineyard for themselves. Eventually they threw him out and killed him.

So far, the meaning of the story is obvious – and fits like a glove with the whole of Luke's gospel. Jesus is the rightful heir to the ancient prophets, and has come to complete their work, challenging Israel one more time to give to the covenant God the honour and obedience that is his due. Israel was charged with bearing the fruit of justice in its own life, and showing God's grace to the world around. But Israel has insisted on keeping the grace for itself, practising injustice in its own life, and seeking to repel and resist the world around by whatever violence might be necessary. Israel has rejected the way of peace, and will now reject its final messenger (19.41–44).

But the story doesn't stop there. The vineyard owner will return at last (Luke has long prepared us for this too), and when he does, the judgment Israel longed to see on the pagan nations will be meted out on it. He will destroy the tenants, and give the vineyard to others. The present regime in Jerusalem, and the self-appointed guardians of Israel's laws and heritage, are signing their own death warrants. Their rejection of Jesus will be taken up by God into the rebuilding plans for his people: 'the stone the builders refused', in this case the Messiah sent to Israel but rejected, 'has become the head cornerstone'.

This quotation from Psalm 118.22 uses a quite different image from that of the vineyard. Imagine a builders' merchant, full of stone ready for the great task. The workers are sorting out the lumps of marble and granite into different sizes and shapes, so they can haul them up to their places on the wall. There is one stone that doesn't belong in any of the groups; they put it over by itself, expecting to throw it out when the job is done. But when they have almost finished, they discover that they need a stone of a particular shape for the very last piece, to round off the top of the corner. There is the stone they rejected earlier. It wouldn't fit anywhere else, but it will fit here.

To quote this verse at this point rams the message home. The workers may reject Jesus now, but they will find that he will be vindicated. He will be seen as the true Messiah. He will build the true Temple, and will himself be its chief feature, the standard by which everything and everyone else is to be judged.

For Reflection or Discussion

Given what happened when Jesus went to Jerusalem, what should we expect to happen when his followers today speak out against injustice? What sort of reaction will the gospel receive when it is announced in places where people use religion (including Christianity) as a means of reinforcing their own privileged position instead of shining God's light into the world?

WEEK 3: SATURDAY

David's Son and the Widow's Mite: Luke 20.41—21.4

[41]Jesus said to them, 'How can people say that the Messiah is the son of David? [42]David himself says, in the book of Psalms,

The Lord says to the Lord of mine
Sit here at my right hand;
⁴³Until I place those foes of thine
Right underneath thy feet.

⁴⁴'David, you see, calls him "Lord"; so how can he be his son?'

⁴⁵As all the people listened to him, he said to the disciples, ⁴⁶'Watch out for the scribes who like to go about in long robes, and enjoy being greeted in the market-place, sitting in the best seats in the synagogues, and taking the top table at dinners. ⁴⁷They devour widows' houses, and make long prayers without meaning them. Their judgment will be all the more severe.'

21 He looked up and saw rich people putting their contributions into the Temple treasury. ²He also saw an impoverished widow putting in two tiny copper coins.

³'I'm telling you the truth,' he said. 'This poor widow has put in more than all of them. ⁴They all contributed into the collection out of their plenty, but she contributed out of her poverty, and gave her whole livelihood.'

'Can you get this balloon into that box?' I asked the little children at the party. The balloon was big, and the box was small. They tried squeezing it in but it wouldn't fit. It kept oozing out through their fingers. One little boy suggested sticking a pin into it, but the others agreed that that was cheating.

Then a little girl, with small, nimble fingers, took the balloon, and undid the knot that was keeping the air inside it. Very carefully she let about half the air out, and quickly tied it up again. Then, with a smile of triumph, she placed the balloon in the box, where it fitted exactly.

That wasn't quite what I'd had in mind, but I had to admit it was clever. Meanwhile, another child had seen the answer. The box was made of cardboard, folded double in places. She unglued two of its sides, and opened it up to its full dimensions. Now the full-size balloon went in perfectly.

Some people, faced with questions like the one Jesus asks about David's Lord and David's son, try to solve it by letting the air out of the balloon. They imagine that God, in order to become human, either stopped being God altogether (the equivalent of a pin in the balloon), or at least shrank his divinity quite severely. The whole New Testament, including Luke, would disagree. For the early Christians, part of the point about Jesus was that the living God was fully and personally present in him, not half present or partly present. What happened in Jesus, and supremely in his death, was the personal action of God himself, not some deputy or demi-god.

The real answer in this case is that the meaning of 'Messiah' is bigger than the Jews of Jesus' day had realized. They were thinking simply of a human king like other human kings, who would fight their battles, rebuild their Temple, and rule with justice. The hints in the prophets and psalms, that when the true king appeared he would be the embodiment of God himself, don't seem to have been picked up at the time. How could they be? The box appeared too small. The balloon wouldn't fit.

Of course, the illustration isn't perfect. Nobody in their right mind would try to get serious theology out of a children's party game. But the question Jesus asked – one of the very few questions he asked, as opposed to the questions other people asked him – went to the heart of explaining what he was doing in Jerusalem, and what his mission was all about.

Much of Luke's gospel has been warning of what will happen if Israel doesn't obey Jesus' kingdom-announcement. Now the psalm Jesus quotes (Psalm 110) speaks of the Messiah as one who will be enthroned until victory is attained over those who have opposed him. The Messiah will be exalted, and judgment will be meted out on those who have chosen the way of violence and injustice. And this Messiah will be one whom David himself, the supposed author of the psalm, does not merely see as a son (and therefore inferior), but as 'my Lord'. The box labelled 'messiahship' is bigger than anyone had realized. It is designed to contain one who will share the very throne of God.

From that point of view, we shouldn't be surprised that the regular human measures of size look misleading and irrelevant. The scribes measure their own value by the length of their robes, the flattering greetings in public, and the places of honour at worship or at dinner. They are living by one scale, but God will measure them by the true one. Privately, they are using their legal skills to acquire legacies from widows who have nobody to speak up for them. Their religion is a sham, and God sees it.

By contrast – another time when the scale of measurement works the opposite way to what people would expect – the poor widow who gave all she had into God's treasury had given more than the rich people who gave what they could easily afford. Back to balloons again: when a small balloon is full of air, the air it releases may only be a small amount, but it leaves the balloon totally flat. Release the same amount of air from a large balloon, and you'll hardly notice the difference.

Putting together these very different stories – Jesus' question about a matter of high theology, and his comment on the scribes and on a poor widow – may seem odd. But the same principle applies to both, and indeed because of that same principle we must insist on holding them together. Because God's way of measuring reality is not our way – because it was always his intention that David's Lord should become David's son – it is also his desire that the same attention be given to the questions of human behaviour and integrity – to matters of 'justice, mercy and the love of God' (11.42) – as we give to the questions of defining and defending the faith.

For Reflection or Discussion

In what ways is religion being used as a cloak for injustice in the world today? What can be done about it?

WEEK 4: A TIME FOR CELEBRATION

FOURTH SUNDAY OF ADVENT

Mary's Song of Praise: Luke 1.39–55

[39]Mary got up then and there, and went in excitement to the hill country of Judaea. [40]She went into Zechariah's house, and greeted Elisabeth. [41]When Elisabeth heard Mary's greeting, the baby gave a leap in her womb. Elisabeth was filled with the holy spirit, [42]and shouted at the top of her voice: 'Of all women, you're the blessed one! And the fruit of your womb – he's blessed, too! [43]Why should this happen to me, that the mother of my Lord should come to me? [44]Look – when the sound of your greeting came to my ears, the child in my womb gave a great leap for joy! [45]A blessing on you, for believing that what the Lord said to you would come true!'

[46]Mary said,

'My soul declares that the Lord is great,
[47]my spirit exults in my saviour, my God.
[48]He saw his servant-girl in her humility;
from now, I'll be blessed by all peoples to come.
[49]The Powerful One, whose name is Holy,
has done great things for me, for me.
[50]His mercy extends from father to son,
from mother to daughter for those who fear him.
[51]Powerful things he has done with his arm:
he routed the arrogant through their own cunning.
[52]Down from their thrones he hurled the rulers,
up from the earth he raised the humble.
[53]The hungry he filled with the fat of the land,
but the rich he sent off with nothing to eat.

> [54]He has rescued his servant, Israel his child,
> because he remembered his mercy of old,
> [55]just as he said to our long-ago ancestors –
> Abraham and his descendants for ever.'

What would make you celebrate wildly, without inhibition?

Perhaps it would be the news that someone close to you who'd been very sick was getting better and would soon be home.

Perhaps it would be the news that your country had escaped from tyranny and oppression, and could look forward to a new time of freedom and prosperity.

Perhaps it would be seeing that the floods which had threatened your home were going down again.

Perhaps it would be the message that all your money worries, or business worries, had been sorted out and you could relax.

Perhaps it would be the telephone call to say that you had been appointed to the job you'd always longed for.

Whatever it might be, you'd do things you normally wouldn't.

You might dance round and round with a friend.

You might shout and throw your hat in the air (I once did that without thinking, before I stopped to reflect what a cliché it was).

You might telephone everybody you could think of and invite them to a party.

You might sing a song. You might even make one up as you went along – probably out of snatches of poems and songs you already knew, or perhaps by adding your own new words to a great old hymn.

And if you lived in any kind of culture where rhythm and beat mattered, it would be the sort of song you could clap your hands to, or stamp on the ground.

Now read Mary's song like that. (It's often called the *Magnificat*, because that is its first word in Latin.) It's one of the most famous songs in Christianity. It's been whispered in monasteries, chanted in cathedrals, recited in small remote churches by evening candlelight, and set to music with trumpets and kettledrums by Johann Sebastian Bach.

It's the gospel before the gospel, a fierce bright shout of triumph 30 weeks before Bethlehem, 30 years before Calvary and Easter. It goes with a swing and a clap and a stamp. It's all about God, and it's all about revolution. And it's all because of Jesus – Jesus who's only just been conceived, not yet born, but who has made Elisabeth's baby leap for joy in her womb and has made Mary giddy with excitement and hope and triumph. In many cultures today, it's the women who really know how to celebrate, to sing and dance, with their bodies and voices saying things far deeper than words. That's how Mary's song comes across here.

Yes, Mary will have to learn many other things as well. A sword will pierce her soul, she is told when Jesus is a baby. She will lose him for three days when he's 12. She will think he's gone mad when he's 30. She will despair completely for a further three days in Jerusalem, as the God she now wildly celebrates seems to have deceived her (that, too, is part of the same Jewish tradition she draws on in this song). All of us who sing her song should remember these things too.

Why did Mary launch into a song like this? What has the news of her son got to do with God's strong power overthrowing the power structures of the world, demolishing the mighty and exalting the humble?

Mary and Elisabeth shared a dream. It was the ancient dream of Israel: the dream that one day all that the prophets had said would come true. One day Israel's God would do what he had said to Israel's earliest ancestors: all nations would be blessed through Abraham's family. But for that to happen, the powers that kept the world in slavery had to be toppled. Nobody would normally thank God for blessing if they were poor, hungry, enslaved and miserable. God would have to win a victory over the bullies, the power-brokers, the forces of evil which people like Mary and Elisabeth knew all too well, living as they did in the dark days of Herod the Great, whose casual brutality was backed up with the threat of Rome. Mary and Elisabeth, like so many Jews of their time, searched the scriptures, soaked themselves in the psalms and prophetic writings which spoke of mercy, hope, fulfilment, reversal, revolution, victory over evil, and of God coming to the rescue at last.

All of that is poured into this song, like a rich, foaming drink that comes bubbling over the edge of the jug and spills out all round. Almost every word is a biblical quotation such as Mary would have known from childhood. Much of it echoes the song of Hannah in 1 Samuel 2, the song which celebrated the birth of Samuel and all that God was going to do through him. Now these two mothers-to-be celebrate together what God is going to do through their sons, John and Jesus.

This is all part of Luke's scene-setting for what will follow, as the two boys grow up and really do become the agents of God's long-promised revolution, the victory over the powers of evil. Much of Mary's song is echoed by her son's preaching, as he warns the rich not to trust in their wealth, and promises God's kingdom to the poor.

But once again Luke hasn't just given us a big picture. Mary's visit to Elisabeth is a wonderful human portrait of the older woman, pregnant at last after hope had gone, and the younger one, pregnant far sooner than she had expected. That might have been a moment of tension: Mary might have felt proud, Elisabeth perhaps resentful. Nothing of that happens. Instead, the intimate details: John, three months before his birth, leaping in the womb at Mary's voice, and the holy spirit carrying Elisabeth into shouted praise and Mary into song.

Underneath it all is a celebration of God. God has taken the initiative – God the Lord, the saviour, the Powerful One, the Holy One, the Merciful One, the Faithful One. God is the ultimate reason to celebrate.

For Reflection or Discussion

When was the last time you had cause to really celebrate? What sorts of events make you want to jump for joy or throw a party?

WEEK 4: MONDAY

Zechariah's Song of Praise: Luke 1.57–80

[57]The time arrived for Elisabeth's child to be born, and she gave birth to a son. [58]Her neighbours and relatives heard that the Lord had increased his mercy to her, and they came to celebrate with her.

⁵⁹Now on the eighth day, when they came to circumcise the child, they were calling him by his father's name, Zechariah. ⁶⁰But his mother spoke up.

'No,' she said, 'he is to be called John.'

⁶¹'None of your relatives', they objected, 'is called by that name.'

⁶²They made signs to his father, to ask what he wanted him to be called. ⁶³He asked for a writing tablet, and wrote on it, 'His name is John.'

Everyone was astonished. ⁶⁴Immediately his mouth and his tongue were unfastened, and he spoke, praising God. ⁶⁵Fear came over all those who lived in the neighbourhood, and all these things were spoken of throughout all the hill country of Judaea. ⁶⁶Everyone who heard about it turned the matter over in their hearts.

'What then will this child become?' they said. And the Lord's hand was with him.

⁶⁷John's father Zechariah was filled with the holy spirit, and spoke this prophecy:

⁶⁸'Blessed be the Lord, Israel's God!
He's come to his people and bought them their freedom.
⁶⁹He's raised up a horn of salvation for us
in David's house, the house of his servant,
⁷⁰just as he promised, through the mouths of the prophets,
the holy ones, speaking from ages of old:
⁷¹salvation from our enemies, rescue from hatred,
⁷²mercy to our ancestors, keeping his holy covenant.
⁷³He swore an oath to Abraham our father,
⁷⁴to give us deliverance from fear and from foes,
so we might worship him, ⁷⁵holy and righteous
before his face to the end of our days.
⁷⁶You, child, will be called the prophet of the Highest One,
go ahead of the Lord, preparing his way,

[77]letting his people know of salvation,
through the forgiveness of all their sins.
[78]The heart of our God is full of mercy,
that's why his daylight has dawned from on high,
[79]bringing light to the dark, as we sat in death's shadow,
guiding our feet in the path of peace.'

[80]The child grew, and became powerful in the spirit. He lived in the wilderness until the day when he was revealed to Israel.

Many people today can't imagine what life would be like without a television. We are so used to it telling us what to think about all the time that, without it, some people become quite worried, lost in a world of their own unfamiliar thoughts like an explorer whose guide has just disappeared. Take away radio, newspapers and smartphones as well, and . . . what would *you* think about all day?

That was the situation, of course, of most people in the world until very recently. It was the situation for everybody in Jesus' time. If you were Zechariah, what would you think of all day?

Your family, certainly. Local village business, presumably. Your health, quite possibly. The state of the crops, the prospect for harvest.

But behind these obvious concerns, there are deeper questions. Something is wrong in the world. People are suffering. *Your* people are suffering. Wicked foreigners have come from far away, with hatred in their eyes and weapons in their hands. Darkness and death have stalked the land. Many people in many countries have had all this to think about over many centuries.

Behind that again, there may be a sense that, though much has gone wrong, somehow there is a larger hope. Things can be put right. Things *will* be put right. Let go of this and you're sunk. Often it's the old people, the ones who cherish old memories and imaginations, who keep alive the rumour of hope.

Zechariah comes across in this passage, especially in the prophetic poem, as someone who has pondered the agony and the hope for many years, and who now finds the two bubbling out of him as he looks in awe and delight at his baby son.

It's a poem about God acting at last, finally doing what he promised many centuries ago, and doing it at a time when his people had had their fill of hatred and oppression. One evil empire after another had trampled them underfoot; now at last God was going to give them deliverance. We can feel the long years of pain and sorrow, of darkness and death, overshadowing his mind. Nameless enemies are lurking round the corner in his imagination and experience.

But we can also feel the long years of quiet prayer and trust. God had made a covenant with Abraham. God had promised to send a new David. God had spoken of a prophet who would go ahead to prepare the way. All these things he had known, believed, prayed and longed for. Now they were all to come true.

Much of the poem could be read simply as the celebration of what we would call a 'political' salvation – though few ancient Jews, and not very many modern ones, would want to separate the secular from the sacred the way the modern West has done. But there are signs that Zechariah's vision goes beyond simply a realigning of political powers.

God's mercy, the forgiveness of sins, the rescue from death itself; all of this points to a deeper and wider meaning of 'salvation'. Luke is inviting us to see that God, in fulfilling the great promises of the Old Testament, is going beyond a merely this-worldly salvation and opening the door to a whole new world in which sin and death themselves will be dealt with.

Zechariah's own story, of nine months' silence suddenly broken at the naming of the child, is a reflection on a smaller scale of what was going on in the Israel of his day. Prophecy, many believed, had been silent for a long time. Now it was going to burst out again, to lead many back to a true allegiance to their God. What had begun as a kind of punishment for Zechariah's lack of faith now turns into a new sort of sign, a sign that God is doing a new thing.

Luke's long first chapter holds together what we often find easier to keep separate. At point after point he has linked his story to the ancient biblical record of Israel, to the patriarchs, kings, prophets and psalms. He is writing of the moment when the centuries-old story was going to come round a corner at last, out of darkness into sudden light. He never forgets this larger perspective; everything that he tells us about Jesus makes sense as the fulfilment of God's ancient promises, the hope of Israel come to fruition at last.

For Reflection or Discussion

Look again at Zechariah's song of praise. Which parts of it do you think offer the most cause for joy and celebration?

WEEK 4: TUESDAY

The Birth of Jesus: Luke 2.1–20

[1]At that time a decree was issued by Augustus Caesar: a census was to be taken of the whole world. [2](This was the first census, before the one when Quirinius was governor of Syria.) [3]So everyone set off to be registered, each to their own town. [4]Joseph too, who belonged to the house and family of David, went from the city of Nazareth in Galilee to Bethlehem in Judaea, David's city, [5]to be registered with his fiancée Mary, who was pregnant.

[6]So that's where they were when the time came for her to give birth; [7]and she gave birth to her firstborn, a son. She wrapped him up and put him to rest in a feeding-trough, because there was no room for them in the normal living quarters.

[8]There were shepherds in that region, out in the open, keeping a night watch around their flock. [9]An angel of the Lord stood in front of them. The glory of the Lord shone around them, and they were terrified.

[10]'Don't be afraid,' the angel said to them. 'Look: I've got good news for you, news which will make everybody very happy. [11]Today a saviour has been born for you – the Messiah, the Lord! – in David's town. [12]This will be the sign for you: you'll find the baby wrapped up, and lying in a feeding-trough.'

[13]Suddenly, with the angel, there was a crowd of the heavenly armies. They were praising God, saying,

[14]'Glory to God in the highest,
and peace upon earth among those in his favour.'

[15]So when the angels had gone away again into heaven, the shepherds said to each other,

'Well then; let's go to Bethlehem and see what it's all about, all this that the Lord has told us.'

[16]So they hurried off, and found Mary and Joseph, and the child lying in the feeding-trough. [17]When they saw it, they told them what had been said to them about this child. [18]And all the people who heard it were amazed at the things the shepherds said to them. [19]But Mary treasured all these things and mused over them in her heart.

[20]The shepherds returned, glorifying and praising God for all they had heard and seen, as it had been told to them.

If you try to point out something to a dog, the dog will often look at your finger instead of at the object you're trying to point to. This is frustrating, but it illustrates a natural mistake we all make from time to time.

It's the mistake many people make when reading the Christmas story in Luke's gospel. What do people know about Jesus' birth? The manger – the Christmas crib. The most famous animal feeding-trough in all history. You see it on Christmas cards. Churches make elaborate 'cribs', and sometimes encourage people to say their prayers in front of them. We know about the animals too, not that Luke even mentions any; the ox and the ass feature prominently in Christmas cards and carols, though there is no indication here either that the shepherds brought their own animals with them, or that there were any in the place where Mary and Joseph were staying.

Let's be clear about where they were lodging. Tradition has them knocking at an inn door, being told there was no room, and then being offered the stable along with the animals. But the word for 'inn' in the traditional translations has several meanings, and it's likely that they were, in fact, on the ground floor of a house where people normally

95

stayed upstairs. The ground floor would often be used for animals – hence the manger or feeding-trough, which came in handy for the baby – but there is nothing to say that there were actually animals there at the time.

To concentrate on the manger and to forget why it was mentioned in the first place is like the dog looking at the finger rather than the object. Why has Luke mentioned it three times in this story?

The answer is: because it was the feeding-trough, appropriately enough, which was the sign to the shepherds. It told them which baby they were looking for. And it showed them that the angel knew what he was talking about. To be sure, it's another wonderful human touch in the story, to think of the young mother finding an animal's feeding-trough ready to hand as a cot for her newborn son. No doubt there are many sermons waiting to be preached here about God coming down into the mess and muddle of real life. But the reason Luke has mentioned it is because it's important in giving the shepherds their news and their instructions.

Why is that significant? Because it was the shepherds who were told *who this child was*. This child is the saviour, the Messiah, the Lord. The manger isn't important in itself. It's a signpost, a pointing finger, to the identity and task of the baby boy who's lying in it. The shepherds, summoned in from the fields, are made privy to the news, so that Mary and Joseph, hearing it from this unexpected source, will have extra confirmation of what up until now has been their own secret.

We have to assume that the shepherds, like other Palestinian Jews at the time, would have known what a saviour, a Messiah, a Lord was to do. In case we need reminding, Luke has introduced the story by telling us about Augustus Caesar, way off in Rome, at the height of his power.

Augustus was the adopted son of Julius Caesar. He became sole ruler of the Roman world after a bloody civil war in which he overpowered all rival claimants. The last to be destroyed was the famous Mark Antony, who committed suicide not long after his defeat at the battle of Actium in 31 BC. Augustus turned the great Roman republic into an empire, with himself at the head; he proclaimed that he had brought justice and peace to the whole world; and, declaring his dead adoptive father to be divine, styled himself as 'son of god'. Poets wrote songs about the new era that had begun; historians told the long story of Rome's rise to greatness, reaching its climax (obviously) with Augustus himself. Augustus, people said, was the 'saviour' of the world. He was its king, its 'lord'. Increasingly, in the eastern part of his empire, people worshipped him too, as a god.

Meanwhile, far away, on that same eastern frontier, a boy was born who would within a generation be hailed as 'son of God'; whose followers would speak of him as 'saviour' and 'lord'; whose arrival, they thought, had brought true justice and peace to the world. Jesus never stood before a Roman emperor, but at the climax of Luke's gospel he stood before his representative, the governor Pontius Pilate. Luke certainly has that scene in mind as he tells his tale: how the emperor in Rome decides to take a census of his whole wide domain, and how this census brings Jesus to be born in the town which was linked to King David himself.

The point Luke is making is clear. The birth of this little boy is the beginning of a confrontation between the kingdom of God – in all its apparent weakness, insignificance and vulnerability – and the kingdoms of the world. Augustus never heard of Jesus of Nazareth. But within a century or so his successors in Rome had not only heard of him; they were taking steps to obliterate his followers. Within just over three centuries the emperor himself became a Christian. When you see the manger on a card, or in church, don't stop at the crib. See what it's pointing to. It is pointing to the explosive truth that the baby lying there is already being spoken of as the true king of the world.

For Reflection or Discussion

What is your favourite part of the Christmas story? What matters most to you about the way we celebrate the birth of Jesus today?

WEEK 4: WEDNESDAY

The Celebration of Jesus: Luke 10.17–24

[17]The seventy came back exhilarated.

'Master,' they said, 'even the demons obey us in your name!'

[18]'I saw the satan fall like lightning from heaven,' he replied. [19]'Look: I've given you authority to tread on snakes and scorpions, and over every power of the enemy. Nothing will ever be able to harm you. [20]But – don't celebrate having spirits under your authority. Celebrate this, that your names are written in heaven.'

[21]Then and there Jesus celebrated in the holy spirit.

'I thank you, father,' he said, 'Lord of heaven and earth! You hid these things from the wise and intelligent, and revealed them to babies. Yes, father, that was what you graciously decided. ²²Everything has been given me by my father. Nobody knows who the son is except the father, and nobody knows who the father is except the son, and anyone to whom the son wishes to reveal him.'

²³Jesus then turned to the disciples privately.

'A blessing on the eyes', he said, 'which see what you see! ²⁴Let me tell you, many prophets and kings wanted to see what you see, and they didn't see it; and to hear what you hear, and they didn't hear it!'

What was it like being Jesus? That's one of the hardest questions for anyone reading the gospels, but this passage gives us some clues.

It's all too easy for Christians to make the mistake of thinking that he just sailed through life with ease; being divine, we sometimes suppose, meant that he never faced problems, never had to wrestle with difficulties. Of course, the gospels themselves give us a very different picture. Yet we can easily be fooled into thinking of Jesus as a kind of Superman.

That sort of understanding might seem, to begin with, to be supported by this passage. Jesus speaks of seeing the satan fall like lightning from heaven. He gives the seventy power over all evil. He celebrates his unique relationship with the father. He speaks of a fulfilment which the great ones of old had longed to see. Surely, we think, this is Jesus the superhero, striding through the world winning victories at every turn, able to do anything at all? And surely, we often think, this Jesus is remarkably irrelevant to our own lives, where we face problems and puzzles and severe tests of faith, where despite our prayers and struggles things often go just plain wrong?

Luke has no intention of describing Jesus as Superman. The rest of his gospel makes that quite clear, and this passage fits in much better with his overall portrait than with the one we project back from our shallow modern culture. What we find here, in fact, is the unveiling of the true nature of the battle Jesus was facing and fighting.

He has now determined to go to Jerusalem, and a new note of urgency comes in as he sends the seventy ahead of him. The depth of this urgency appears in the discussion, with the seventy, of their role and mission. Jesus began his public career with a private battle against the real enemy; this battle will continue until its last great showdown, as the powers of darkness gather for their final assault (22.53).

We must remind ourselves who or what 'the satan' is in Jewish thinking. The word 'satan' literally means 'accuser', and 'the satan' appears in scripture as the Director of Public Prosecutions in God's heavenly council (Job 1.6–12; 2.1–7; Zechariah 3.1–2). At some point he seems to have overstepped the role, not only bringing unfounded accusations, but inciting people to do things for which he can then accuse them. Finally, in flagrant rebellion against God and his plans of salvation for the world, the satan seeks to pervert, distort and overthrow Israel, the chosen bearers of God's promise, and to turn aside from his task Israel's true Messiah, the bringer of fulfilment. He has gained enormous power because the world in general, and Israel's leaders too, have been tricked by his cunning.

Jesus' task is therefore not simply to teach people a new way of life; not simply to offer a new depth of spirituality; not simply to enable them to go to heaven after death.

Jesus' task is to defeat the satan, to break his power, to win the decisive victory which will open the way to God's new creation in which evil, and even death itself, will be banished.

So what did Jesus see, and what did it mean? 'I saw the satan fall like lightning from heaven,' he said. As the seventy were going about their urgent mission, Jesus in prayer had seen a vision, echoing the prophetic visions of the downfall of the ancient enemy (Isaiah 14.4–23; Ezekiel 28.1–19). Jesus had seen, in mystical sight, the heavenly reality which corresponded to the earthly victories won by the seventy. He knew, and could assure the seventy, that their work was indeed part of the great victory begun in the desert and to be completed on the cross. They must not imagine, though, that they can now sit back and enjoy their new powers. What matters is that God's purpose is going forward, and that they are already enrolled in it. There is shortly coming a time, after all, when even the Twelve, even Peter, will be sifted like wheat by the satan, before the final victory can be accomplished (22.31–32).

In the same moment of vision and delight, Jesus celebrates what he realizes as God's strange purpose. If you needed to have privilege, learning and intelligence in order to enter the kingdom of God, it would simply be another elite organization run for the benefit of the top people. At every stage the gospel overturns this idea. Jesus sees that the intimate knowledge which he has of the father is not shared by Israel's rulers, leaders and self-appointed teachers; but he can and does share it with his followers, the diverse and motley group he has chosen as his associates. God, says St Paul, chose what is foolish in the world to shame the wise, the weak to shame the strong.

As Jesus goes on his way to fight the final battle in Jerusalem, he knows that this strange purpose is already being accomplished. At its heart is the creation of a new people: a people who recognize Jesus as God's true son, the Messiah, and a people who through the work of Jesus are coming to know God for themselves as father. A people, in other words, who fulfil Israel's destiny; a people who see and hear what prophets and kings longed to see and hear but did not.

For Reflection or Discussion

What does Jesus' prayer of celebration tell us about his relationship with his father? And what encouragement do you draw from this as one of his present-day disciples?

WEEK 4: THURSDAY

The Parable of the Great Banquet: Luke 14.12–24

[12]He then turned to his host. 'When you give a lunch or a supper,' he said, 'don't invite your friends or your family or relatives, or your rich neighbours. They might ask you back again, and you'd be repaid. [13]When you give a feast, invite the poor, the crippled, the lame and the blind. [14]God will bless you, because they have no way to repay you! You will be repaid at the resurrection of the righteous.'

[15]One of the guests heard this, and commented, 'A blessing on those who eat food in God's kingdom!'

[16]Jesus said, 'Once a man made a great dinner, and invited lots of guests. [17]When the time for the meal arrived, he sent his servant to say to the guests, "Come now – everything's ready!" [18]But the whole pack of them began to make excuses. The first said, "I've just bought a field, and I really have to go

and see it. Please accept my apologies." [19]Another one said, "I've just bought five yoke of oxen, and I've got to go and test them out – please accept my apologies." [20]And another one said, "I've just got married, so naturally I can't come." [21]So the servant went back and told his master all this. The householder was cross, and said to his servant, "Go out quickly into the streets and lanes of the town and bring in here the poor, the crippled, the lame and the blind." [22]"All right, master," said the servant, "I've done that – but there's still room." [23]"Well then," said the master to the servant, "go out into the roads and hedgerows and make them come in, so that my house may be full! [24]Let me tell you this: none of those people who were invited will get to taste my dinner."'

Once, many years ago, I preached a sermon on this passage. I emphasized the extraordinary way in which Jesus tells his hearers to do something that must have been as puzzling then as it is now. Don't invite friends, relatives and neighbours to dinner – invite the poor and the disabled. The sermon had a strange effect. In the course of the next week my wife and I received dinner invitations from no fewer than three people who had been in church that day. Which category of guest we came into we were too polite – or anxious – to ask.

It looks as if the passage is offering real advice. The parable of the supper, which follows, is a parable all right, but Jesus really seems to have intended his hearers to take literally his radical suggestion about who to invite to dinner parties. Social conditions have changed, of course, and in many parts of the world, where people no longer live in small villages in which everyone knows everyone else's business, where meals are eaten with the doors open and people wander to and fro at will (see 7.36–50), it may seem harder to put it into practice. Many Christians would have to try quite hard to find poor and disabled people to invite to a party – though I know some who do just that. Nobody can use the difference in circumstances as an excuse for ignoring the sharp edge of Jesus' demand.

In particular, they cannot ignore it in the light of the parable. The story is, obviously, about people who very rudely snub the invitation to a splendid party. They make excuses of the usual kind. The householder, having gone to all the trouble of organizing and paying for a lavish feast, is determined to have guests at his table, even if he has to find them in unconventional locations. The original guests have ruled themselves out, and others have come in to take their place.

The first level of meaning of this parable should be clear. Jesus has been going around Galilee summoning people to God's great supper. This is the moment Israel has been waiting for! At last the time has arrived; those who were invited long ago must hurry up now and come! But most of them have refused, giving all kinds of reasons. But some people have been delighted to be included: the poor, the disadvantaged, the disabled. They have come in and celebrated with Jesus.

The second level, as with the previous parable, is what this might mean for Luke in particular. Once again the expected guests are the Jews, waiting and waiting for the kingdom, only to find, when it arrived, that they had more pressing things to occupy them. Of course, in Luke's day many Jews had become Christians. The detail of the parable can't be forced at this point: it isn't true, at this level, that 'none of those who were invited shall taste my banquet', since clearly many Jews were part of Jesus' kingdom-movement from the beginning. But the majority of the nation, both in Palestine and in the scattered Jewish communities in the rest of the world, were not. Instead, as it must have seemed to those first Jewish Christians, God's messengers had gone out into the roads and hedgerows of the world, getting all kinds of unexpected people to join in the party – not just Gentiles, but people with every kind of moral and immoral background, people quite different from them culturally, socially, ethnically and ethically.

But there is a third twist to this parable, in which it bends back, as it were, on itself, returning to the challenge which Jesus gave in verses 12–14. The party to which the original guests were invited was Jesus' kingdom-movement, his remarkable welcome to all and sundry. If people wanted to be included in Jesus' movement, this is the sort of thing they were joining.

Once again, therefore, the challenge comes to us today. Christians, reading this anywhere in the world, must work out in their own churches and families what it would mean to celebrate God's kingdom so that the people at the bottom of the pile, at the end of the line, would find it to be good news. It isn't enough to say that we ourselves are the people dragged in from the country lanes, to our surprise, to enjoy God's party. That may be true; but party guests are then expected to become party hosts in their turn.

For Reflection or Discussion

How do you celebrate God's kingdom in your life? How might you or your church become a party host and share the good news more widely in the way described by Jesus in this parable?

WEEK 4: FRIDAY

The Parable of the Prodigal: Part 1
The Father and the Younger Son: Luke 15.11–24

[11]Jesus went on: 'Once there was a man who had two sons. [12]The younger son said to the father, "Father, give me my share in the property." So he divided up his livelihood between them. [13]Not many days later the younger son turned his share into cash, and set off for a country far away, where he spent his share in having a riotous good time.

[15]'When he had spent it all, a severe famine came on that country, and he found himself destitute. [15]So he went and attached himself to one of the citizens of that country, who sent him into the fields to feed his pigs. [16]He longed to satisfy his hunger with the pods that the pigs were eating, and nobody gave him anything.

[17]'He came to his senses. "Just think!" he said to himself. "There are all my father's hired hands with plenty to eat – and here am I, starving to death! [18]I shall get up and go to my father, and I'll say to him: 'Father; I have sinned against heaven and before you; [19]I don't deserve to be called your son any longer. Make me like one of your hired hands.'" [20]And he got up and went to his father.

'While he was still a long way off, his father saw him and his heart was stirred with love and pity. [21]He ran to him, hugged him tight, and kissed him. "Father," the son began, "I have sinned against heaven and before you; I don't deserve to be called your son any longer." [22]But the father said to his servants, "Hurry! Bring the best clothes and put them on him! Put a ring on his hand, and shoes on his feet! [23]And bring the calf that we've fattened up, kill it, and let's eat and have a party! [24]This son of mine was dead, and is alive again! He was lost, and now he's found!" And they began to celebrate.'

We might think that the parable of the prodigal son, as it's usually known, hardly needs an introduction. It has inspired artists and writers down the years. Rembrandt's famous painting, with the younger son on his knees before the loving and welcoming father, has become for many almost as much of an inspiration as the story itself. Phrases from the story – the 'fatted calf', for instance, in the King James version of the Bible – have become almost proverbial.

And yet. People often assume that the story is simply about the wonderful love and forgiving grace of God, ready to welcome back sinners at the first sign of repentance. That is indeed its greatest theme, which is to be enjoyed and celebrated. But the story itself goes deeper than we often assume.

Let's be sure we've understood how families like this worked. When the father divided the property between the two sons, and the younger son turned his share into cash, this must have meant that the land the father owned had been split into two, with the younger boy selling off his share to someone else. The shame that this would bring on the family would be added to the shame the son had already brought on the father by asking for his share before the father's death; it was the equivalent of saying 'I wish you were dead'. The father bears these two blows without recrimination.

To this day, there are people in traditional cultures, like that of Jesus' day, who find the story at this point quite incredible. Fathers just don't behave like that; he should (they think) have beaten him, or thrown him out. There is a depth of mystery already built in to the story before the son even leaves home. Again, in modern Western culture children routinely leave homes in the country to pursue their future and their fortune in big cities, or even abroad; but in Jesus' culture this would likewise be seen as shameful, with the younger son abandoning his obligation to care for his father in his old age. When the son reaches the foreign country, runs through the money, and finds himself in trouble, his degradation reaches a further low point. For a Jew to have anything to do with pigs is bad enough; for him to be feeding them, and hungry enough to share their food, is worse.

But of course the most remarkable character in the story is the father himself. One might even call this 'the parable of the Running Father': in a culture where senior figures are far too dignified to run anywhere, this man takes to his heels as soon as he sees his young son dragging himself home. His lavish welcome is of course the point of the story: Jesus is explaining why there is a party, why it's something to celebrate when people turn from going their own way and begin to go God's way. Because the young man's degradation is more or less complete, there can be no question of anything in him commending him to his father, or to any other onlookers; but the father's closing line says it all. 'This my son was dead and is alive; he was lost and now is found.' How could this not be a cause of celebration?

Inside this story there is another dimension which we shouldn't miss. One of the great stories of Israel's past was of course the exodus, when Israel was brought out of Egypt and came home to the promised land. Many years later, after long rebellion, Israel was sent into exile in Babylon; and, though many of the exiles returned, most of Jesus' contemporaries reckoned that they were still living in virtual exile, in evil and dark days, with pagans ruling over them. They were still waiting for God to produce a new exodus, a liberation which would bring them out of their spiritual and social exile and restore their fortunes once and for all. For Jesus to tell a story about a wicked son, lost in a foreign land, who was welcomed back with a lavish party – this was bound to be heard as a reference to the hope of Israel. 'This my son was dead, and is alive'; ever since Ezekiel 37 the idea of resurrection had been used as picture-language for the true return from exile.

Yes, says Jesus, and it's happening right here. When people repent and turn back to God – which, as we've seen, meant for Jesus that they responded positively to his gospel message – then and there the 'return from exile' is happening, whether or not it looks like what people expected. His answer to the Pharisees and other critics is simple: if God is fulfilling his promises before your very eyes, you can't object if I throw a party to celebrate. It's only right and proper.

There is a danger in splitting the story into two, as we've done. The second half is vital, and closely interwoven with the first. But in this first section the emphasis is on the father's costly love. From the moment he generously gives the younger son what he wanted, through to the wonderful homecoming welcome, we have as vivid a picture as anywhere in Jesus' teaching of what God's love is like, and of what Jesus himself took as the model for his own ministry of welcome to the outcast and the sinner.

For Reflection or Discussion

How would you describe the thoughts and feelings that the father in this story would have experienced in response to the younger son's actions? Why, when the son returns, does the father respond with celebration rather than with anger and recrimination?

WEEK 4: SATURDAY

The Parable of the Prodigal: Part 2
The Father and the Older Son: Luke 15.25–32

[25]'The older son was out in the fields. When he came home, and got near to the house, he heard music and dancing. [26]He called one of the servants and asked what was going on.

[27]'"Your brother's come home!" he said. "And your father has thrown a great party – he's killed the fattened calf! – because he's got him back safe and well!"

[28]'He flew into a rage, and wouldn't go in.

'Then his father came out and pleaded with him. [29]"Look here!" he said to his father, "I've been slaving for you all these years! I've never disobeyed a single commandment of yours. And you never even gave me a young goat so I could have a party with my friends. [30]But when this son of yours comes home, once he's finished gobbling up your livelihood with his whores, you kill the fattened calf for him!"

[31]'"My son," he replied, "you're always with me. Everything I have belongs to you. [32]But we had to celebrate and be happy! This brother of yours was dead and is alive again! He was lost, and now he's found!"'

A vivid phrase from a schoolboy poem, written by a class-mate of mine over 30 years ago, remains with me to this day. He described a park-keeper whose job was to pick up litter on a spiked pole. Surrounded by the glorious beauty of flowers and trees, with the sun sparkling through the leaves, he only had eyes for the rubbish he had to collect, and the damage it did. The lines I remember sum up his plight:

> 'Destroys the nature in this park, litter,' he said, without
> Lifting his head.

He could only see the bad, and was blind to the beauty.

That sums up the older brother in the story. And it's the older brother who provides the real punchline of the parable. This is Jesus' response to his critics. They were so focused on the wickedness of the tax-collectors and sinners, and of Jesus himself for daring to eat with them despite claiming to be a prophet of God's kingdom, that they couldn't see the sunlight sparkling through the fresh spring leaves of God's love. Here were all these people being changed, being healed, having their lives transformed physically, emotionally, morally and spiritually; and the grumblers could only see litter, the human rubbish that they normally despised and avoided.

The portrait of the older brother is brilliantly drawn, with tell-tale little shifts of phrase and meaning. 'Your brother', says the servant, 'has come home'; but he won't think of him like this. 'This son of yours,' he says angrily to his father. 'This your brother,' says the father, reminding him gently of the truth of the matter. 'I've been slaving for you,' he says to his father, whereas in fact they had been working as partners, since the father had already divided his assets between them (verse 12). Everything the father has belongs to him, since the younger brother has spent his share; and that, presumably, is part of the problem, since the older brother sees all too clearly that anything now spent on his brother will be coming out of his own inheritance.

The phrase which ties the story to Jesus' opponents comes out tellingly: 'I've never disobeyed a single command of yours.' That was the Pharisees' boast (compare Philippians 3.6); but the moral superiority which it appears to give melts like snow before the sunshine of God's love. Where resurrection is occurring – where new life is bursting out all around – it is not only appropriate, it is *necessary* to celebrate (verse 32). Not to do so is to fail to meet generosity with gratitude. It is to pretend that God has not after all been at work. It is to look only at the rubbish and to refuse to smell the flowers.

In terms of what God was doing in Israel through Jesus, we can see once more that the new kingdom-work which was going forward was indeed like a return from exile. Sinners and outcasts were finding themselves welcomed into fellowship with Jesus, and so with God, in a way they would have thought impossible. But whenever a work of God goes powerfully forward, there is always someone muttering in the background that things aren't that easy, that God's got no right to be generous, that people who've done nothing wrong are being overlooked. That happened at the time when the exiles returned from Babylon; several people, not least the Samaritans, didn't want them back.

This story reveals above all the sheer self-centredness of the grumbler. The older brother shows, in his bad temper, that he has had no more real respect for his father than his brother had had. He lectures him in front of his guests, and refuses his plea to come in. Once more the father is generous, this time to his self-righteous older son. At this point we sense that Jesus is not content simply to tell the grumblers that they're out of line; he too wants to reason with the Pharisees and the lawyers, to point out that, though God's generosity is indeed reaching out to people they didn't expect, this doesn't mean there isn't any left for them. If they insist on staying out of the party because it isn't the sort of thing they like, that's up to them; but it won't be because God doesn't love them as well.

This parable points, for Luke, beyond the immediate situation of Jesus' ministry and into the early church. There, Gentiles were coming into the church, and Jews and Jewish Christians often found it very difficult to celebrate the fact. Equally, as Paul realized when writing Romans, it was vital that the new communities never gave the impression to their older brother that God had finished with him. Somehow the balance must be kept.

The story is, of course, unfinished. We naturally want to know what happened next. How will the younger brother behave from now on? What arrangements will they make? Will the two sons be reconciled? Sometimes when a storyteller leaves us on the edge of our seats like this it's because we are supposed to think it through, to ask ourselves where we fit within the story, and to learn more about ourselves and our churches as a result.

For Reflection or Discussion

Which role in this story do you find comes most naturally to you? How can we celebrate the party of God's love in such a way as to welcome not only the younger brothers who have come back from the dead, but also the older brothers who thought there was nothing wrong with them?